JUSTICE
IN
BAGHDAD

JUSTICE
— IN —
BAGHDAD

A MEMOIR OF
LAW, SERVICE, AND
INTEGRITY

LESLIE CAYER OHTA

SUMMIT PRESS
Publishers

Printed in the United States of America
First Printing, 2026
ISBN: 979-8-9939104-3-7
Library of Congress Number: 2026914452

Summit Press Publishers
P.O. Box 1356
Intervale, New Hampshire 03845

For information about special discounts available for bulk purchase, please contact author@summitpresspublishers.com.

To my dad, who encouraged me to
march to my own drummer.

TABLE OF CONTENTS

CHAPTER 1

THE EMAIL THAT CHANGES EVERYTHING

The fluorescent lights hummed overhead in the ordinary Department of Justice rented building in Washington, D.C., where I sat at my ordinary government desk, clicking through ordinary emails on an ordinary Tuesday afternoon. After six years working on the most extraordinary case of my career—an $8 billion contract dispute over a Navy stealth airplane that never got built—I was back to the reality of a Government Contracts branch attorney.

For six years, the case had been everything I loved about Federal work—complex, high-stakes, intellectually challenging, and with real national security implications. Tremendous autonomy, cutting-edge technology, the intersection of defense contracting and commercial litigation—Lockheed's F-117 Stealth, Northrop Grumman's B-2 Bomber. But now my input in the litigation was over, and I found myself in a professional dead space, wondering what meaningful work might come next.

Then I saw it. An email from the Attorney General himself, marked with the kind of urgent priority that makes you sit up straighter in your wheeled office chair.

Seeking experienced attorneys for a one-year deployment to Iraq. The Justice Department Criminal Branch's Overseas Prosecutorial Development Program. Rule of law reconstruction efforts.

This wasn't one of those routine administrative emails that usually got buried in management layers. The Attorney General had apparently given specific orders: this goes directly to the line attorneys. We're looking for people who actually do the work. I'd learned over the years that many of these requests for volunteer assignments never made it past the U.S. Attorneys—they had staff to manage, cases to prosecute, and didn't want their best people getting ideas about adventure elsewhere. But this was different. This was important enough that the usual gatekeeping had been bypassed.

Ten seconds. That's all it took. I read the description once, maybe twice, and something clicked into place with the satisfying certainty of a puzzle piece finding its proper spot.

I knew I could do it. No, needed to do it.

I didn't pause to consider the implications. Didn't weigh pros and cons or make a list of reasons why a sixty-six-year-old federal prosecutor might not be the ideal candidate for a war zone deployment. I simply clicked reply and typed: "I'm interested."

The certainty shouldn't have surprised me, but it did. After all, I'd spent decades making calculated legal arguments, carefully weighing evidence, and methodically building cases that could withstand appellate scrutiny. But this decision bypassed all of that analytical machinery. It came from someplace deeper, someplace that had been quietly accumulating experiences for four decades.

I forwarded the email to my family with a brief note: "Applied for this. Looks fascinating."

The response was swift and unanimous horror.

"Why would you leave your beautiful house in Annapolis?" my son Cary asked when I called, and I could hear the bewilderment in his voice—the way you might react if someone announced they were trading in their comfortable sedan for a motorcycle and a sleeping bag. "You have this great job, great travel opportunities. Why would you want to do that?"

He had a point about the house. It was perched on a peninsula—not a gated community, exactly, but one of those rare neighborhoods with only one way in and out. Our community owned the beaches. There was a marina, an impressive clubhouse, a swimming pool, and a guest house in the back. I'd spent around $600,000 on renovations and improvements. It was the kind of place people dream about retiring to.

But that was exactly the problem. I wasn't ready to retire to anything.

My kids thought I was crazy, that I didn't fully appreciate the possible "hardships" or "danger." I'd never been the type to agonize over how my decisions would affect my family the way many women of my generation did. During law school, I studied twelve hours a day. My husband Toshi, who saw parenting as a mother's job, had to bring our two toddlers to the daycare center, pick them up, bring them home, bathe them, feed them, and get them to bed. When I left to study in Southeast Asia for ten weeks, it was my sister Joanne who took care of the boys and gave them a soft lap to sit on. That wasn't me. They were two and three years old. When I came back, I'm not sure Miki, the younger one, even recognized me.

Even when Cary and Miki were older, I'd sent them to overnight camp in the Shenandoah Mountains for eight weeks each summer because I was traveling constantly for work. I'd felt guilty about it then, driving two hours to visit them at hotels on weekends, only to learn later that the two boys would have preferred I skip the visits so they could focus on horseback riding, riflery, and swimming.

Maybe I was selfish. I know I'm very driven, very competitive. I like battles. I like being challenged. I like to win. Some would say compulsive about productivity. Back home, among many things, I'd been a competitive skier—won the Connecticut State Championship for downhill, slalom, and giant slalom my sophomore year of high school. I'd learned something important at the Junior National Training Camp that I was invited to attend: I wasn't willing to sacrifice everything else to be the absolute best at one thing. I was a jack-of-all-trades, a master of none. But whatever I did, I needed to be doing something, measuring progress, seeing results.

I don't hear the word "no"—not unless it comes with a reason—never have.

I was three and a half years old. For my sister Marilyn's fifth birthday party, the family gathered in the backyard. My mother was going to buy ice cream, and I wanted to go with her. She said, "No, go back to the backyard." Then she drove away.

I knew about cars. I knew I couldn't catch up. But I followed anyway, walking a long, long way before anyone noticed

I was missing. Eventually, a police car found me. They drove me home to the party.

I don't remember being reprimanded. I wasn't punished. No one said, "Don't ever do that again." They just brought me home.

That's just who I am.

I've always believed that certain characteristics are *immutable*—hardwired into us from birth and unchangeable. My sister Marilyn is brilliant—two master's degrees and a PhD in biology—but she could sit in her seat and never raise her hand, never comment, never push back. She could just endure. I couldn't. I had to speak out, had to act, had to go. Neither of us chose our temperament. We just came that way.

I always told my kids, "Don't boast about your innate characteristics, because you didn't earn them. Those are *immutable*—intelligence, temperament, where you were born, what you were born into."

But other qualities are *mutable*—things you choose, things you build. Honesty. Trustworthiness. Hard work. Those are what we should judge people by. The rest is just luck: a gift or a curse, but never something you earned or deserved.

Seems my kids were missing something fundamental about who I'd become over the years. This wasn't a sudden departure from character—it was the logical next step in a life that had been preparing for this moment without me fully realizing it.

The timing couldn't have been better, actually. My marriage to Toshi had ended years earlier—not in rancor, but with the quiet recognition that we'd always been two independent people who'd happened to share a home and children. Both my sons were grown men now— Cary still worried about his mother's latest adventure— and Miki was building his own life in Germany with his wife and their daughters. I had no one depending on me for daily care, no one whose routine would be disrupted by my absence. Though even when I had, I'd found ways around that.

At sixty-six, I was also uniquely positioned professionally. My legal career was established beyond question—beginning with my acceptance into the Attorney General's Honors Program. The Honors Program was particularly significant—acceptance required being at the top of your law school class, writing for Law Review, and achieving the highest bar exam scores. I'd tied with one other person for the highest score on the Connecticut bar exam. It was intensely competitive, and most people used it as a steppingstone to a high-paying private practice after three years. The fact that I'd never left said something about what motivated me.

I knew my value on the open market. There would be opportunities waiting upon my return. That security gave me a freedom that younger attorneys, still building their reputations, couldn't afford.

But more than career considerations, this opportunity connected to something deeper about my relationship with the rule of law itself. I'd spent three decades in federal service because I believed in the necessity of ensuring that justice is meted out fairly, even within imperfect systems. Democracy wasn't just a political theory to me—it was a framework that allowed truth to emerge through fair processes, transparent institutions, and the protection of individual rights. Iraq represented a chance to help foster and rebuild those institutions, to plant seeds that might grow into something meaningful long after American troops went home.

The truth was, I felt a sense of responsibility. We'd invaded two countries, changed their political structures, and now needed to follow through. But Iraq was different from Afghanistan in one crucial respect: we'd gone in unilaterally, without international consensus, without exhausting alternatives, and without a plan for what came after. That failure put us morally on the hook in a way that political expediency alone couldn't account for. We owed it to the Iraqi people to do it right.

Despite hitting a single button and applying to both the Afghanistan and Iraqi programs, I leaned toward Iraq — Afghanistan had a reputation, I would later hear, for being medieval, a warring collection of fiefdoms with nothing underneath. At least Iraq had national laws on the books. What I didn't yet fully grasp was just how overwhelming the challenges would be if I wound up in Iraq. The Iraq I was volunteering for wasn't just a country rebuilding; it was one where the very concept of justice had been systematically destroyed, and where American efforts to help often felt like shouting into a hurricane of cultural, security, and programmatic impediments that could crush even the most determined optimism.

By 2010, Iraq was a country still reeling from three decades of brutal dictatorship followed by seven years of chaotic reconstruction. Saddam Hussein had been pulled from his spider hole in 2003—a narrow hole six to eight feet deep, covered with a rug, bricks, and dirt—tried in proceedings so dangerous that defense lawyers were assassinated, and executed in 2006. But his legacy remained: a nation with weak democratic institutions, no tradition of judicial independence, no experience with constitutional law. The evidence rooms in Baghdad held 26 million documents detailing systematic oppression—handwritten orders for mass killings, instructions to crush Kurdish minorities, and records of torture chambers where Olympic athletes were caged for weeks by Saddam's son.

The new Iraqi government was attempting to build a democracy from scratch in a country where the previous system had been based entirely on fear, patronage, and violence. They had courtrooms but judges who'd never operated independently. They had law schools but no tradition of legal advocacy. They had prisons full of children as young as eight.

This was the Iraq that needed help—not a country tweaking an existing system, but one trying to invent democratic governance while still surrounded by the rubble of totalitarianism. Where intellectuals, doctors, and academics were routinely assassinated, creating a brain drain that crippled efforts at institutional rebuilding. Where trafficking in persons had become an epidemic. Where armed violence continued to kill approximately two hundred Iraqi civilians every month.

I grew up the daughter of a man who was contemptuous of lawyers. This wasn't casual dislike—my father had a principled objection to the entire profession. "You go to a lawyer with a problem, and you tell the lawyer you want him to say 'yes' or you want him to say 'no,'" he'd explain. "The lawyer really doesn't care. As long as he gets paid, he'll say 'yes,' or he'll say 'no.'"

The irony, of course, is that I'd never intended to become one of those lawyers my father distrusted. But life has a way of leading you places you never planned to go.

My mother died when I was seven. When I was eight, my father married a nurse with a daughter named Joanne, who was the same age as me. We were in the same grade, shared a bedroom, and were the best friends ever. My father had built a career that took him from a ninth-grade education to the superintendent of a major company. He taught us that formal credentials mattered less than character and capability, that you could survive things that seemed impossible if you learned to adapt and get on with it. We were raised with a very strong ethic of truth and veracity. That's why we gravitated to science—because science may not always get the answer, but to get there, you follow the truth. Facts, testing, experimentation. My father couldn't fathom being an attorney, defending someone regardless of the truth, simply because one is paid to advocate.

That "adapt-and-get-on-with-it" lesson served me well when I joined the Peace Corps and discovered that the world operated on entirely different assumptions than the ones I'd grown up with. The head of the chemistry department at my college had MIT connections and had gotten me a position there—unusual for someone straight out of undergrad. My father was so proud. For him, MIT was the epitome of scholarship, everything formal education could mean. I told him I was going to the Peace Corps for two years first, then MIT. Of course, that never happened. I went to the Philippines instead, expecting to build water-sealed toilets in villages and help communities address their basic needs. Instead, they'd sent me to teach chemistry and physics at the laboratory high school on the campus of the University of the Philippines and to work part-time developing chemistry curriculum materials in the Graduate School of Education—not exactly the grassroots experience I'd envisioned, but service nonetheless. I'd never wanted to be a teacher, but I discovered I actually loved it. The mission had stayed the same even when the circumstances changed: "Go where you're needed, contribute what you can, make things better than you found them."

Teaching turned out to be a form of cultural bridge-building—helping people understand not just scientific concepts but ways of thinking that crossed international boundaries.

Living in Japan for years post-Peace Corps also taught me that you could navigate completely foreign systems without compromising your core principles.

When I returned to the States from Japan, I found another environment that fed that same hunger for truth. UConn Health Center was one of the first medical schools in the country with a full-time lawyer and a full-time philosopher on the tenured teaching faculty—people asking hard questions about the ethics of what medicine was doing and what it should be doing. I took a position coordinating the first two years of the medical-dental program, a made-up title for work no one had done before, and I became good friends with both of them. The arrangement let me take any seminar I wanted. I chose human experimentation—learning about transgender medicine fifty years before most Americans had heard the term. The same curiosity that had drawn me to chemistry, the same commitment to following truth wherever it led, found a home in those seminars where nothing was settled and everything was being questioned.

By the time I ended up in law school—almost by accident—I'd already learned to build bridges across cultural divides, to work within systems I didn't fully understand, to find purpose in places where others saw only chaos.

The Justice Department offered me something private practice couldn't: thirty years of never saying a word in a courtroom that I didn't passionately believe. At DOJ, we don't represent individual clients. We don't represent agencies. We represent the United States of America. That meant when I appeared in court, I was speaking my truth—my own analysis of the law. It's about being excellent in what you do, having integrity, and doing justice. Only at the Justice Department would I have had that freedom. More importantly, it offered "details"—temporary assignments that allowed attorneys to leave their offices for up to one year wherever they were needed most.

This details system was central to why I'd stayed at the Justice Department for three decades instead of jumping to private practice like most Honors Program graduates. I'd entered DOJ straight out of my clerkship at the Connecticut Supreme Court, assigned to the Torts Branch in Washington, where I spent four years defending the government in vaccine injury cases arising from the 1976 Swine Flu immunization program—the one where President Ford rolled up his sleeve on national television. It was complex, multi-district litigation: medical malpractice, products liability, wrongful death claims filed in federal courts across the country.

After four years, I moved to the U.S. Attorney's Office in Connecticut, trading Washington for New Haven, civil defense work, and criminal prosecution. That's where I built the forfeiture program. Eleven years later, I returned to Main Justice—back to the Civil Division, now handling government contract disputes.

The Department understood that keeping talented attorneys long-term meant providing varied experiences, challenging assignments, and opportunities to grow beyond the routine work of representing federal agencies. They actively encouraged people to volunteer for projects that weren't directly related to their home offices because it prevented boredom and developed expertise that ultimately benefited the entire system.

The assignments had been remarkable, including Bosnia for election monitoring in the aftermath of the war. The Organization for Security and Cooperation in Europe found me through my Peace Corps background—they were looking for former volunteers. I went to my supervisor and said I'd like to do this as a volunteer. It was a ten-week program. I was willing to use my vacation time, but they said no—we'll give you leave. You don't have to use your own time. Two separate trips: six weeks for voter registration, then back for ten days during the actual election.

During the first Bosnia assignment, I had a significant case pending—a big law firm on the other side. We had a telephone status conference, and I told the judge I needed a ten-week break. The opposing counsel started ranting. "Justice can just assign another attorney. This isn't—" The judge, a woman with a reputation for being extremely rigid, lit into them like you wouldn't believe. She recognized the importance of what I was doing. Their case was simple—at the end, their client would either get money or not. That's all it was about. What I was doing mattered more.

That moment made me feel recognized. Valued. Significant.

The leave situation happened more than once. I was also asked to assist the U.S. Marshals Service, which had a role in the $80 million assistance package given to Bogotá to wage the war on drugs. A year defending Immigration Judges' decisions, writing briefs, and arguing asylum appeals. Each time, DOJ made accommodations—leave, advanced leave, whatever it took. It's one of the reasons I stayed at the Justice Department for thirty years. They let me merge my volunteer activities with my job.

Each assignment taught me something new about operating under pressure, maintaining professional composure in crisis, and building trust with people who had every reason to be suspicious of American intentions.

There were smaller assignments I could have volunteered for, too, like the opportunity for attorneys to volunteer for temporary duty in Puerto Rico. The Assistant U.S. Attorneys there didn't want to prosecute their fellow citizens for trespassing on federal bombing ranges during protests, so requests went out to all U.S. Attorneys' offices. These were easy cases—trespassing is trespassing, especially when you're walking on government property during bomb testing—but they gave newer attorneys valuable litigation experience while helping resolve politically sensitive situations.

Based on the pattern, I believe the Justice Department encouraged these assignments to keep people engaged and growing. It was a brilliant retention strategy that had kept me interested and challenged for all those years. Each detail had prepared me for something bigger, built skills I didn't know I'd need, and created a network of international experience that would prove invaluable in Iraq.

By the time the Attorney General's email arrived, I'd been to forty-eight countries. I'd monitored elections in societies trying to rebuild after conflict. I'd worked with people who lived under constant threat, who risked everything just by talking to Americans. I'd learned to navigate corruption diplomatically, to find common ground across vast cultural differences, to maintain hope when institutions failed.

Most importantly, I'd discovered something about myself: I'm drawn to places where systems are broken, and people need help figuring out how to fix them. I don't need clear metrics of success or tidy resolution. I just need to know that the work matters.

And the decision carried weight.

I understood why. This wasn't a training exercise or a diplomatic courtesy call. This was about helping a country build democratic institutions from scratch, populated by people, at least in Iraq's case, who'd lived under dictatorship for decades and had little experience with constitutional law or judicial independence. They needed teachers, mentors, cultural interpreters—people who could help them understand not just what democracy looked like, but how it actually functioned in practice.

The one-year limit was nonnegotiable. Federal regulations prohibited any government employee from remaining in a war zone for more than 365 days. I would return exactly one year after I left, whether the work was finished or not. That constraint made the decision easier—this wasn't a permanent life change, just an intense sabbatical in which to apply my legal experience to one of the most challenging reconstruction efforts in modern history.

I would be working as a Resident Legal Adviser with the Provincial Reconstruction Team in Baghdad, part of the Overseas Prosecutorial Development Assistance and Training (OPDAT) program—a Criminal Division initiative designed to strengthen foreign criminal justice institutions. Since 1991, OPDAT had placed attorneys in over thirty-seven countries, providing technical assistance to help establish fair and transparent justice systems. In Iraq, that meant everything from assessing criminal justice institutions to training law enforcement personnel to helping construct prisons that met international standards.

Still, I understood my family's alarm. I was sixty-six years old, a grandmother of five from Connecticut, volunteering for deployment to a country where people got killed for talking to Americans. The government would make a significant investment in each person they sent—they weren't going to waste that kind of money on someone who couldn't handle the physical and psychological demands.

That investment amount wasn't an abstract figure. It represented extensive training, security clearances, medical preparation, weapons certification, psychological evaluation, and months of preparation for a reality none of us could fully imagine. They needed to be absolutely certain that each person they selected could not only survive the assignment but contribute meaningfully to the mission.

But as I sat in that fluorescent-lit office, staring at the Attorney General's email, none of those future challenges seemed daunting. They seemed like problems to be solved, systems to be navigated, skills to be acquired.

I'd been solving problems like this my whole life. If anything went wrong, if this adventure didn't work out, I'd land on my feet. At this stage of my life, I could afford to choose significance over comfort, purpose over security.

"I know I can do it," I told my son when he called back, still hoping I'd come to my senses.

He didn't understand. The house, the artifacts, the entertaining—those were things I'd enjoyed. But they weren't who I was.

The certainty hadn't wavered in the hours since I'd hit send on my reply. If anything, it had grown stronger. This wasn't about proving anything to anyone or seeking adventure for its own sake. This was about service—the kind of meaningful work that had drawn me to the Peace Corps decades earlier.

Here was a chance to matter again in ways that went beyond litigating civil and criminal cases on behalf of the DOJ. To use everything I'd learned about cultural bridge building, about working within broken systems, about maintaining integrity under pressure. To help people who genuinely needed what I had to offer.

My father had raised us to follow truth wherever it led, to make decisions based on facts rather than fears. The fact was simple: I was uniquely qualified for this assignment. I had the legal expertise, international experience, cultural adaptability, and temperament for working in challenging environments.

Most importantly, I had something that couldn't be taught or screened for: a deep belief in the possibility of justice, even in the most imperfect systems. Even when institutions failed, even when politics corrupted good intentions, individual relationships could transcend boundaries. Small acts of bridge-building could plant seeds of change.

Iraq mattered. The work mattered. And I could do it.

The office around me—with its ordinary desk and ordinary emails and ordinary afternoon light—suddenly felt like the launching pad it had always been. Not a place to settle into comfort, but a platform for the next challenge.

I picked up the phone to call the personnel officer about the application timeline. There was work to do.

CHAPTER 2

VETTING THE WARRIOR

The U.S. Government wasn't taking any chances with its $1.3 million investment.

That figure would have echoed in my mind as I prepared for the panel interview had I known it at the time. They couldn't afford to waste that investment on someone who would crack under pressure or quit after weeks, proving to be an embarrassment to the U.S. by leaving unfinished missions with the Iraqis.

The screening process existed to eliminate those risks. Every question would be designed to predict how I'd perform when mortars were falling, the temperature was 120 degrees, and some Iraqi judge was testing whether this American woman really understood anything about his country's legal system.

The vetting process had begun weeks earlier, though "process" overstates what it was. I was in the Jizera Mountains of the Czech Republic—on an Earthwatch expedition to collect water samples from acid-rain-damaged headwaters—when I received word to call Andrew, the Iraq program manager. Andrew was in Iraq at the time. I was on a mountainside. I found a signal, made the call, and answered his questions.

That was my first interview for the deployment. Neither of us seemed to find the geography unusual.

The interview was scheduled for three hours. Six Justice Department officials would place me under a microscope and evaluate me. I'd faced juries, argumentative opposing counsel, and questioning district court and appellate judges for thirty years, but something about this felt different. More consequential. These people would decide whether I'd get the chance to test everything I thought I knew about myself against the reality of a war zone.

They'd have access to my complete file—not just performance evaluations and case outcomes, but the stack of awards I kept stored in a cupboard somewhere in my house. More importantly, the panel deciding whether to make me an offer would have access to all of my yearly evaluations and my trial record.

My trial record spoke for itself—in thirty years, I could count my losses on one hand. Some were reversed on appeal—that happens—but my success rate spoke to careful case review and thorough preparation. Justice Department attorneys were expected to carefully and thoroughly examine the merits of the Government's exposure and to settle or try cases as appropriate. I didn't take on a case unless I believed in it completely and could prove it convincingly.

That wasn't just professional pride talking. I'd spent thirty years drawing a line and never crossing it. Three times during my career, supervisors had asked me to take positions I disagreed with. Each time, I'd gone to the U.S. Attorney and said, "I'm sorry, but I can't do that." Each time, the case was reassigned to someone else. No conflict, no drama—just a professional recognition that some attorneys had lines they wouldn't cross, and I was one of them.

They'd also see the case that had consumed the last six years of my career: an $8 billion contract dispute over a stealth airplane the Navy had paid for and never received—at the time, the largest case ever filed against the United States government.

I'd gotten that one the same way I got most things: a phone call I hadn't expected. Joan—the most brilliant attorney I'd worked with at DOJ—called out of the blue. "The biggest case ever filed against the United States needs your help." I told her I knew nothing about military aviation, nothing about stealth technology, nothing about the contractors involved. She said, "You're ideal for this."

I flew to Washington, took the interview, and said yes. For six years, I assembled and led the scientific and technical case, recruiting expert witnesses who were the chief designers of the F-117 Stealth Fighter and the B-2 Bomber, men who'd spent entire careers in top-secret and special-access programs, whose families never knew where they went or when they'd be back. When I needed someone who could make aeronautical engineering comprehensible to a jury, a colleague suggested Bill Nye the Science Guy. I'd never heard of him. I looked him up, called his office repeatedly, got no response, flew to Seattle, and showed up at his studio unannounced while he was filming his last Disney segment. He came out, took me to lunch, and agreed to consult for $100 an hour and not charge for his airfare or hotel, since he often traveled to D.C. or stayed at the

L'Enfant Plaza Hotel, given that his brother was the general manager there.

The panel would understand what that case demonstrated. It wasn't the subject matter they'd be looking at. It was the pattern: know nothing about it, say yes, figure it out. I'd been operating this way since I was a kid.

At St. Thomas Aquinas, a Catholic high school where compliance was the highest virtue, I was the nail that kept getting hammered down. When the geometry teacher—a Latin teacher pressed into service—made calculation errors, I raised my hand and corrected her. I got zeros for the day, but I couldn't let a wrong answer stand. When a civics teacher railed against certain forms of government, I spoke up and said that people had the right to self-determination, that they should be able to choose for themselves the forms of government they wanted. She paused, then told the class that if someone was trying to lead them astray politically, they should avoid that person. She was clearly referring to me. The Latin teacher assigned us to memorize a page of the dictionary every night—a learning method I found absurd. I just didn't do it, collecting zeros and fifties all semester. Then we took the *Auxilium Latium*, a nationwide Latin exam, and when the teacher read aloud the names of the highest scorers, she came to mine and stopped. "Well, clearly there's been an error here," she said. "I'm going to have to check on that." There was no error. I knew the Latin. I just studied it my own way, accepting the fact that learning foreign languages didn't come easily to me.

That kind of integrity had cost me nothing professionally because my work spoke for itself.

Each panel member would have carefully studied my file. Their questions would likely go beyond what was written in performance reviews to probe motivations, decision-making processes, and stress responses. What they no doubt wanted to understand was whether those achievements predicted success in a completely different environment. They wanted to see how I handled pressure in person.

They understood that psychological screening had essentially already happened—I'd been filling out detailed background forms for twenty years, and they had comprehensive records of my mental health, financial stability, and potential vulnerabilities. Can you be bought by the enemy? Are you in debt? Do you have a drug problem? Is there something in your past that could be used against you? They're not just asking if you can handle stress. They're asking if you can be compromised. But there would be more, which is what they'd be after with their line of questioning.

When I sat before them, the members of the interview panel explained that they were interested specifically in my experience handling criticism under fire. I had shifted in my seat. Was that why they'd chosen this as their first area of exploration?

I'd earned my living speaking in courtrooms, so the interview format felt familiar despite the unusual stakes. This was just another judge or jury to convince, another case to present clearly and persuasively. I knew immediately where to go.

The drug forfeiture cases I took on as an AUSA had taught me something valuable about operating when everyone was watching and judging—and getting the story wrong.

Asset forfeiture was one of the most powerful tools in the War on Drugs, and I'd helped build Connecticut's program from the ground up. Congress had passed a statute allowing local police departments to bring drug forfeiture cases to federal agencies—usually the DEA, FBI, and IRS. If we litigated successfully, 90 percent of whatever we recovered went back to that local department. At the time, federal agents got credit for the tons of marijuana or pounds of cocaine they seized, not the cash or property. So, a DEA agent and I traveled around the state, meeting with police departments and explaining, "You bring us the case, we'll litigate it, and you get 90 percent back if we are successful." Over forty police departments signed on. The program worked because the system worked—multiple decision-makers, judicial oversight at every step, checks and balances designed to ensure fairness.

Then came the Derbacker case, and with it, a lesson in how thoroughly the media could distort a story.

The DEA had been tracking a major drug dealer for years. His son—a small-time dealer himself—lived with his elderly parents in a modest ranch house. When local police executed a search warrant at the house, they found drugs scattered throughout the home. Not hidden. Scattered. There was marijuana in a mug on the kitchen shelf. Marijuana was in the drawer where the grandmother kept her towels. Cocaine in her underwear drawer. Drugs on the bedside table. The grandson's bedroom had drugs everywhere and money scattered across the floor. In the front hall closet sat a suitcase full of marijuana, and on the shelf right above it, an OHAUS scale—the kind used in chemistry labs or to weigh drugs. Twenty-two guns and a wooden crate of ammunition were seized from the home.

At trial, I had everything in the courtroom—the twenty-two guns, the wooden crates of ammunition with their long gold and yellow bullets, the suitcases of marijuana, the OHAUS scales. The drugs had been bagged and sealed as evidence, then placed back in the suitcases. I surreptitiously slit those bags. I wanted the court to smell the marijuana.

These grandparents weren't oblivious. They had loaned their son $50,000. They knew exactly what was happening under their roof. I offered them the opportunity to take a polygraph, which was my standard practice. I informed everyone claiming to be "an innocent owner" that if they passed the polygraph questions regarding their lack of knowledge of these drug activities, we'd return their property. My colleague in the FBI's polygraph unit and I had traveled to a number of local and out-of-state law enforcement entities to lecture on this approach: use the polygraph to separate the truly innocent from those who knew. The grandparents refused to take the test. They could have. We would have explored whether they were afraid of their son or grandson, whether fear explained their silence. But they didn't want to answer those questions.

The grandson's behavior after his arrest only confirmed what we already knew about the family's situation. He made bail, went to his girlfriend's house with a ladder, climbed to the second floor, and set the whole place on fire. Sometime later, he dressed in a black ninja costume, got on his motorcycle—we'd seized his car—and held up a gas station with a crossbow (because I'd seized all twenty-two of his guns). This was not a family of innocent bystanders caught up in someone else's crimes.

But that's not the story the media told.

CBS approached me about a proposed segment on Ed Bradley's *Street Stories*. The U.S. Attorney's Office authorized my participation. Reporters came to a bar in New Haven where attorneys, FBI, and DEA agents gathered on Friday nights. They interviewed my colleagues, looking for someone to say I'd gone too far.

When the Associated Press called, I was given rare permission to speak—prosecutors typically weren't allowed to talk to the press; we drafted press releases—the DOJ made the decisions whether to release them—and let the work speak for itself. I tried to explain the system. Local police bring evidence of drug trafficking to federal agencies. Agents evaluate the case and bring it to me. I assess the merit. If appropriate, I seek authority from the U.S. Attorney to pursue forfeiture. If authorized, I will prepare a seizure warrant for a U.S. magistrate's signature. The property owner is notified of the seizure warrant and how to contest it at a probable cause hearing. Cases go to trial. Appeals follow. Every step involves multiple decision-makers and judicial oversight. I wasn't some rogue attorney "running amok." I was an attorney working within a system designed to ensure fairness—a system that consistently upheld our actions because they were legally sound.

The AP reporter wrote that "Leslie Ohta boasted she never lost a case."

He'd completely missed the point. I wasn't boasting. I was explaining that the system worked—that multiple people reviewed every decision, that courts consistently upheld our actions because the process was rigorous and the evidence was solid. But nuance doesn't make headlines.

Years later, I discovered that Bill Bryson had written about me in his book *I'm a Stranger Here Myself.* He used my name—spelled it out, O-H-T-A—and held me up as an example of everything wrong with American drug policy. He wrote that I had "made a name for herself by seizing the property of almost anyone even tangentially connected with a drug offense—including a couple in their eighties whose grandson was found to be selling marijuana out of his bedroom." He claimed they "had no idea" their grandson had marijuana in the house and "of course had nothing to do with it themselves." He called it "zealous vindictiveness."

I cry at love scenes, happy endings, and unkind moments in movies—anything emotional, the tears will come. That's why I was and am such a big reader; I can cry in private. But if somebody says something nasty to me in real life? That's different. I won't give them the satisfaction.

Bryson never called me. Never asked about the cocaine in the grandmother's underwear drawer. Never mentioned the refused polygraph. Never noted that the family's own son was a major drug dealer the DEA had been tracking for years, or that the grandson committed arson and armed robbery after his arrest. He took the story he wanted to tell and told it, facts be damned.

Most lawyers say bad press is good press. I wasn't like most lawyers. I had spent my entire career refusing to say anything in a courtroom I didn't believe. I had lines I wouldn't cross.

Being publicly maligned by a bestselling author who hadn't done his homework—having my character attacked based on a story he'd gotten wrong—was intolerable. Not because I wanted fame or feared controversy, but because I had too much integrity to accept a lie told in my name.

The first time I heard the phrase "junkyard dog" was at an FBI conference. The agent in charge of the Connecticut field office was introducing me to a large group of agents. He was singing my praises, talking about the forfeiture program's success, and then he said, "This is Leslie Ohta. She's our junkyard dog." What I didn't know was that it was meant to be highly complimentary.

I was mortified. I'd never heard the expression before. All I heard was *dog*—a word that, applied to women, rarely meant anything good. I stood there in front of all those agents, thinking, *What an insulting, repulsive, derogatory name.*

What I learned from all of it was this: you can do everything right and still be vilified. You can follow every procedure, obtain every approval, win every appeal, and still have your character assassinated in the national press. You can offer polygraphs to prove innocence and have your fairness ignored. You can explain the system until you're hoarse, and a reporter can reduce it to bragging. You can be named Prosecutor of the Year by the people who actually understood your work and still be called a zealot by people who never bothered to learn the facts.

The forfeiture work taught me to operate when everyone was watching and judging. It taught me that integrity doesn't protect you from criticism—it only ensures you can live with yourself when it comes. It taught me that some people will always see what they want to see, and the best you can do is know the truth yourself. Those were exactly the skills Iraq would require.

"Tell us about your experience working in post-conflict societies," one panelist asked after she'd taken copious notes. The others leaned forward attentively.

I knew the Bosnia experience would be most relevant, so I offered them that story. In the summer of 1997, I'd been recruited by the Organization for Security and Cooperation in Europe (OSCE) to work as an adjudicator in Brčko, Republic of Srpska—the most contested area in postwar Bosnia. They'd found me through Peace Corps volunteer lists, and deliberately so. Between the Dayton Peace Accords and the upcoming municipal elections, there wasn't time to train election workers from scratch. The OSCE had made a calculated decision: former Peace Corps volunteers had already undergone the kind of cross-cultural, high-pressure preparation the assignment required. My job was to determine which displaced refugees were eligible to vote. The work required interviewing displaced people, examining documents, and making decisions that carried real political weight in a region still raw from ethnic cleansing.

It was a violent atmosphere. American forces, UN forces—nobody could carry weapons. They only had billy clubs. And into that, I uncovered fraud in the voter registration process. When we reported it, Sarajevo shut down the entire program. We had to start over from scratch—void everything, rebuild the system. I wrote the training manual for the new process, supervised staff, and monitored every step to ensure compliance with the rules. In a separate case, I investigated the politically motivated firing of a local election official; my report led the OSCE to order her reinstatement.

But Bosnia wasn't where my preparation had begun.

Even before they could ask, I volunteered further evidence because I understood what they were looking for: that I fit the bill. They were gauging how easily I would quit in the face of inevitable complications. And complications came in all guises: the mundane, the cultural, and in-your-face threats.

The Peace Corps had understood this long before the Justice Department did. Seven hundred volunteers had been selected for the Philippines that year, split between two training sites. My group was part of an experiment in "self-deselection"—they wanted people to quit during training rather than after arriving in-country, thereby avoiding embarrassment to the United States government.

The psychiatric evaluations for that post had been particularly intense. "What would you do if it rained for thirty days?" the psychiatrist would ask. "Read a book." "You don't have any books." "Listen to the radio." "You don't have a radio." As someone with a science background, these hypothetical scenarios seemed ridiculous—but I understood what they were testing: psychological resilience, adaptability, the ability to function when normal coping mechanisms disappeared.

Twenty-five percent of our group self-deselected during those ten weeks of training. The strategy worked—once we got to the Philippines, almost nobody left early. The government had learned it was better to lose people during preparation than to invest heavily in someone who would wash out after a month and create an international incident.

That Peace Corps experience taught me to navigate cultural differences diplomatically. Not just the dramatic examples like going bat hunting in a Philippine swamp, then eating the catch, but the smaller, daily negotiations that required understanding people whose assumptions were at times completely different from mine.

The University of the Philippines provided a small four-room house on its campus. Busy with our teaching, my housemate and I hired a local woman to help with cleaning, paying her well by local standards. One day, we noticed she was wearing my roommate's blouse—not borrowed, but taken. In America, the solution would be straightforward: confront her, demand it back, and probably fire her. In the Philippines, that approach would have humiliated her publicly and marked us as arrogant Americans who didn't understand face-saving protocols.

Instead, we said nothing. The blouse wasn't worth creating conflict over, and we understood that she probably didn't think about property the same way we did. We continued working together successfully. It was a small lesson in choosing battles wisely and recognizing that different cultural frameworks required different responses. Those skills would prove invaluable in Iraq, where similar diplomatic sensitivity would be required daily.

But there was another experience the panelists seemed to consider: my time in Bogotá during the height of Colombia's drug war. They asked a question about it, and I gave them the relevant details.

It was the 1980s, and Congress had allocated $80 million for the war on drugs. I'd obviously become well known in the asset forfeiture community—that specialized area of prosecution where you don't just go after the criminals, like the Derbacker kid, you go after their money and property. That expertise earned me a spot on a DOJ team sent to educate Colombian officials about asset forfeiture laws and how they could be used as powerful weapons against the cartels.

I expounded, told them about the group of us arriving in Bogotá, thinking we were attending a standard international legal seminar. The government housed us in this beautiful old hotel—elegant architecture, lovely accommodations. We couldn't believe they'd put us somewhere so nice. Then one day, about twenty-five American soldiers showed up at the front door, straight out of the jungle in filthy fatigues, weapons at the ready. That's when we realized: the hotel was owned and guarded by the U.S. government. We weren't guests. We were assets being protected.

Every evening, they'd make elaborate arrangements for us—like taking us in a tramway up a mountain to a restaurant. Usually, government officials don't treat their attorneys like VIPs. But we understood quickly that the special treatment wasn't about making us comfortable. It was about keeping us alive. They didn't want to scare us, but Bogotá was very, very unsafe.

The thing was, Bogotá wasn't making headlines the way Iraq later would. Most Americans had no idea what was happening there, except maybe that five members of Colombia's Supreme Court had recently been murdered. Pablo Escobar was systematically killing government officials who opposed him. Our Colombian counterparts—the prosecutors and law enforcement officials we were training—were meeting with us at tremendous personal risk. I had enormous respect for them. They knew that collaborating with Americans made them targets, yet they showed up anyway.

We held the first session in Bogotá, working with them on asset forfeiture legislation that could dismantle the cartels' financial infrastructure. Then we flew them all to Miami for a second session, partly for their safety, partly because we weren't allowed to go shopping or sightseeing in Colombia. The security protocols were that strict.

The panelists before me considered the Bogotá experience carefully. I'd already operated in a war zone. I'd already worked with armored vehicles, armed escorts, and secure housing. I'd already collaborated with foreign officials under threat. I understood what it meant to function professionally when the backdrop was violence, and the stakes were life and death.

They paused to pour themselves glasses of water and exchange a few sidebar comments. Then one of them asked, "What motivates you to volunteer for this assignment?"

That was the crucial question. I told them about never taking a legal position I didn't believe in, about choosing meaningful work over higher compensation. I wasn't running away from anything—I was running toward the chance to apply decades of legal expertise to one of the most challenging reconstruction efforts in modern history.

This seemed to satisfy them, so they finished up with a few questions that covered practical considerations. They asked about my security clearances, which I held at the highest levels, including special access for military programs. I'd traveled on a diplomatic passport for a case involving Ukraine—had to go to Moscow to interview a witness. They told me not to show the diplomatic passport. "Use your regular one," they instructed. "You're going to be photographed and watched, but they might not bug your room if they think you're just a tourist."

The lead panelist, a woman whose manner suggested she'd conducted these interviews many times, leaned forward. "We've never had a candidate as strong as you are for this position," she said. "Where have you been? Why haven't you volunteered before?"

I explained that I'd never known about most of these opportunities and that the Attorney General's direct email was unusual for reaching line attorneys rather than being filtered through management layers. I didn't mention that my supervisors in commercial litigation weren't happy about losing me. I was a highly productive attorney, so leaving for a year was disruptive. All my cases would have to be reassigned, and deadlines would have to be waived.

Near the end, they asked about physical preparation. I assured them I'd approach fitness requirements systematically, the same way I'd approached every other professional challenge. They seemed impressed by my methodical attitude—this wasn't someone seeking adventure or running from personal problems, but a professional preparing seriously for a difficult assignment.

The conversation wound down with logistics about the training process: four months of preparation, covering everything from cultural briefings to medical training to weapons proficiency. To carry a Glock in Iraq, I'd need to qualify with it—and first be sworn in at the U.S. Marshals office as a deputy U.S. Marshal, with the weapon restricted to self-protection only, Iraq only. Even the gun came with a brief. It would be intensive, designed to transform comfortable federal attorneys into people capable of operating effectively in a war zone.

"We'll be in touch within a week," the lead panelist said.

Walking out of the building that afternoon, I felt cautiously optimistic. The panel had asked tough questions, but nothing I couldn't answer convincingly. Most importantly, they seemed to understand that I was approaching this decision seriously, with realistic expectations about the difficulties involved and a track record of performing under pressure.

***

The brief psychiatric screening process that followed proved almost comically perfunctory. When I entered the designated office, I sat in the chair in front of the desk. The woman conducting the evaluation suggested I'd be more comfortable on the sofa next to her. It struck me as odd, but I went along with it. She started asking questions about my background, but when I mentioned that I'd studied eight languages—Esperanto, Latin, German, French, Filipino (Tagalog), Japanese, and Spanish—and that I'd traveled to forty-eight countries, cataloging the details, she essentially ended the session. "Thank you very much. Goodbye."

I understood what had happened. She was professionally screening for psychological instability, unrealistic expectations, and inappropriate motivations. They were very worried about mental health, much, much more so than physical safety. I'd be living in a fortress where there were no couples, no children, no pets, for months on end. We'd see no normal signs of life, like people riding their bikes or zipping to the store. They needed to weed out the people who couldn't deal with isolation, or who would create problems when under stress, or who would crack and ask to go home. They needed people who could focus and get the job done without a lot of drama.

The selection call came five days later. I was in my office when the phone rang.

"Congratulations, you've been selected for deployment to Iraq," the familiar voice said. "Are you ready to begin the training process?"

"Yes," I said without hesitation.

"Training starts next month. Four months of preparation, then one year in Baghdad. You'll be working as a Resident Legal Advisor with the Provincial Reconstruction Team, focusing on judicial reform and legal system development. Any questions at this point?"

"No questions. I'm ready."

After hanging up, I sat quietly for several minutes, absorbing the reality that would now unfold. What they didn't need to say was that, while training, I would be expected to carry my full caseload.

But first, I had immediate work to do. If I were going to represent American interests in Iraq, I believed I needed to be in the best physical condition of my adult life. I had, in fact, already started. The Czech expedition had been classified very active. Worried about keeping pace with the group, I'd joined

24-Hour Fitness and hired a personal trainer named Rob. I was never left behind on the mountain. When Iraq came into focus, I went back to Rob. The interview had made it clear that physical demands could be significant, and I wasn't going to let fitness limit my effectiveness.

The transformation I was planning would be dramatic—a complete restructuring of my physical capabilities to match the demands of operating in a war zone. That work would begin immediately and require the same systematic approach I'd applied to every other professional challenge.

During those months ahead, I would also need to complete the psychological transition from comfortable federal trial attorney to someone preparing for a war zone where none of my accumulated awards and recognition would matter. I'd have to prove myself all over again, in conditions far more challenging than any courtroom.

As the formal training period approached, I felt ready. Not because I understood everything that lay ahead—that would have been impossible—but because I'd prepared systematically for the unknown. The foundation was already solid, and the intensive preparation ahead would build the specific technical skills needed for success.

The vetting process was complete. Whatever Iraq presented, I'd meet it the same way I'd met every other significant challenge—with careful preparation, absolute commitment, and the confidence that comes from never having said a word in court I didn't passionately believe. If that made me a junkyard dog, then Iraq was about to get one with thirty years of legal experience behind me. I was ready for the fight.

CHAPTER 3

TRAINING FOR THE UNTHINKABLE

After decades of federal litigation, I recognized a comprehensive legal defense strategy when I was living through one. Every session, every skill, every piece of equipment would serve double duty—keeping us safe while creating documentation that no one could later fault. This strategy included weapons training, medical training, psychological evaluation, cultural preparation, and signed acknowledgments of known risks. I approached it all with frank appreciation for the bureaucratic logic.

Every weekday morning at 5:30 AM, I met with my personal trainer. This wasn't optional feel-good fitness; this was mission-critical preparation. I thought I needed to be strong enough to carry 40 pounds of protective equipment through Baghdad heat, fit enough to move quickly when situations turned dangerous, and disciplined enough to maintain peak performance under sustained stress.

The early morning sessions were brutal: strength training, cardiovascular conditioning, and endurance work.

My weight had crept up over the years—a natural consequence of a career spent in airports and conference rooms, of loving good food and beer, of prioritizing work over exercise. It wasn't dramatic weight gain, just the slow accumulation that happens when you're focused on cases and travel and building a career rather than maintaining peak physical condition.

I'd done Earthwatch expeditions before—including a recent one in the Czech Republic, archaeological digs with my sister Marilyn in Thailand, meerkat projects in South Africa, and an elephant conservation project in Kenya—and these always specified the level of physical fitness required for each project. I approached the Iraq deployment the same way: it would be like an Earthwatch expedition, but longer and more dangerous, requiring a higher level of fitness than most Earthwatch projects.

While my trainer put me through increasingly demanding routines, I'd mentally prepare for the workday ahead—the cases I needed to move forward, the meetings scheduled, the normal business of a Justice Department attorney handling litigation that couldn't stop just because I was preparing for deployment.

After each workout, I'd shower, dress in my usual professional attire, and head to the office to maintain my existing caseload. The duality felt perfectly natural—preparing my body for war zone deployment while keeping my legal cases active. I thrived on the intensity, the demanding schedule, the clear sense of purpose driving every decision.

The physical transformation was remarkable. I lost 50 pounds in three months—enough to earn a spot on the gym's bulletin board, with my before-and-after pictures posted for everyone to see among the gym's most successful weight-loss achievements. I'd always been competitive, even when there wasn't an official contest. Especially when there wasn't an official contest. If someone were going to post weight loss achievements, mine would be at the top of the list.

It cost me a fortune on a government salary, even at the top of the pay scale—five days a week with a personal trainer—but I was used to making what I earned stretch so I could live the life I wanted. I'd been at the bottom of the federal pay scale when I first joined the Department of Justice. Back then, I'd been accepted into the Honors Program—you had to be at the top of your class, have written for *Law Review*. It was a real distinction. I'd also gotten a clerkship, so they gave me a one-year waiver. Then I was accepted to Harvard and Yale for graduate work, but the DOJ wouldn't grant me another waiver. So, I decided to go to D.C. with the kids. Toshi stayed in Connecticut, where he worked in the company that had employed my father.

Those four years were wonderful but also really difficult. In Washington, I was traveling constantly—mostly within the U.S., but I also had to go overseas, to Europe and Australia. That meant I needed live-in help. During the academic year, it wasn't so bad—I'd get a college student, basically room and board and a small salary. But in the summers, I had to send both kids away to camp for those guilt-ridden eight weeks.

The disciplined approach to my physical training worked. I gained strength, developed the kind of stamina that would no doubt prove essential for surviving Baghdad's relentless climate and security demands, and demonstrated to myself that I could master this level of preparation while maintaining my professional responsibilities.

***

Next came the official medical training. "We don't teach CPR," the instructor announced on day one. "If someone next to you is in cardiac arrest, you let them die. Your job is to save the people you can save." This wasn't callousness; it was battlefield triage logic. In mass-casualty situations, resources were directed to those most likely to survive with intervention.

Instead, we learned tourniquets. Lots of tourniquets. How to apply them to ourselves, how to help someone else apply theirs. The black nylon tourniquet straps would hang from our bulletproof vests alongside our names and blood types. Practical accessories for an impractical assignment.

The training felt familiar in ways that might have surprised my fellow trainees. Death and I had been acquainted for a long time.

As kids, my sister Marilyn and I had a laboratory in our basement. We did experiments on mice—four cages of them—exposing them to cigarette tar, to ultraviolet light, and other substances. We did taxidermy. I made skeletons. Two girls with a chemistry set and no squeamishness, poking at the mechanics of life and death before we were old enough to find it strange.

During the Peace Corps, a summer assignment sent me to Mindanao, the southernmost part of the Philippines, to work as a physician's aide at a rural health clinic. I lived with a doctor and his family. My bedroom opened directly off the living room—and in that living room sat an open casket. A wake. It lasted days. I slept feet away from a dead body night after night, because that's what the family did, and I was their guest. It wasn't traumatic. It was just how things were done.

Years later, after returning to the U.S. from Japan, I worked as an administrative coordinator at UConn Health Center, coordinating the first two years of the medical-dental program. Part of my job was attending autopsies with the students, carrying smelling salts and barf bags. These were young people just out of college. Many had never even been to a wake. They'd see their first autopsy and go pale, reach for the wall, and need help staying upright. I'd found the clinical precision oddly comforting.

I also had my own cadaver to dissect—a rejected corpse, a grossly overweight male, my silent study partner. I lost interest in him after a few short weeks, but not before he taught me more about the human body than any textbook could. The process was methodical: identify structures, understand systems, appreciate the remarkable engineering that keeps us alive until it doesn't. Death, when approached systematically, lost much of its emotional weight.

That experience had taught me something valuable about mortality—it was a technical problem to be understood, not a mystery to be feared. The Iraq medical training drew on the same mindset. Arterial bleeding here, tourniquet placement there. Compress this, stabilize that. If you approached the human body as a system of problems with technical solutions, the emotional component became manageable.

***

After medical basics came the bulletproof vest fitting. The Personal Protective Equipment, or PPE, weighed forty pounds. The Kevlar plates had to be stored on special cross-shaped racks to prevent damage. The vest itself was personalized with our names and blood types prominently displayed.

Looking at that vest—my name printed clearly across the chest, my blood type ready for quick identification—made the abstract reality of danger concrete. This wasn't theoretical preparation. Someone had calculated exactly what information emergency medical personnel would need if they found me unconscious and bleeding.

The vest was designed to be equipped with everything we might need to survive long enough for help to arrive: tourniquets, a flashlight, a knife, shrapnel-resistant goggles, and Nomex gloves. Each item had been selected based on careful analysis of what had actually saved lives in previous deployments.

***

The weapons training was another source of particular satisfaction. I'd handled guns before—when I was doing firearms cases at the Justice Department, the agents made us train at the range. When you're in a courtroom with guns on the table, picking them up, showing them to the jury, you need to feel comfortable. Shotguns, pistols—we'd shot all kinds. But that was years ago, and qualifying to carry a nine-millimeter Glock in a war zone was a different matter.

The NRA instructors had one day to get me certified. The technique that nearly defeated me was called the monkey grip. You fire your six shots, then shift your hand so your thumb pushes the lever that releases the magazine—it drops, your other hand is already at your belt, grabbing the next one, and it's in within seconds. One smooth motion.

I couldn't do it. My hands wouldn't cooperate. I had to use my other hand to push the release lever, then grab the magazine separately—losing four or five seconds each time. The whole qualifying test lasted two minutes and twenty seconds, and you don't know the sequence in advance. The instructor didn't think I'd pass.

During the final two-minute qualifying test, the instructor said, "Prone position, center mass." I flung myself to the ground and fired. I then heard murmuring behind me. "Who's Granny with a gun?" If someone was going to call me Granny, I'd be the most competent, best-trained Granny they'd ever encountered. I learned to disassemble, clean, and reassemble weapons. I practiced until my accuracy scores impressed the instructors. I understood the mechanics, the safety protocols, and the legal framework governing the use of force.

The irony was perfect: a federal attorney learning to shoot straight so she could teach constitutional law in a war zone. I found the precision appealing in the same way I'd always been drawn to legal analysis—clear rules, measurable outcomes, skills that improved with practice and attention to detail.

Cross-cultural training, held at the State Department over several weeks, provided the intellectual preparation for our mission—understanding history, customs, religion, social dynamics, and language. This felt like familiar territory to me.

In the Philippines, we'd go to barrio fiestas—we were Peace Corps, we stood out, we were always invited. At one fiesta, little puppies were running around, and I mentioned how cute they were. One of the kids pointed to the stew I was eating and said, "Yeah, you're eating the mom." I was fastidious about food back then. But you eat what's offered. It's their country, their culture. You're not going to do something unethical, but you're also not going to insult your hosts by refusing their hospitality.

I'm glad I went through that experience. It stood me in good stead when I traveled to Africa or anywhere else—the understanding that being a guest means accepting the world as your hosts live in it, not as you think it should be.

Some cultural misunderstandings had far more impact. Lifelong impact. Case in point: When my Peace Corps service in the Philippines ended, my friend Linda and I planned to travel together. I'd been playing tennis with a Japanese student at the University of the Philippines, and during one conversation, I mentioned our plans. He said his father had fought in the Philippines during the war and felt terrible about what he'd done. They had a guest house behind their main house. We could stay there—six months, maybe a year. His father wanted to repay something. It was more about Linda's connection, her being Filipino.

We thought it was a genuine invitation. We didn't understand that in Japanese culture, people often say things to please you without real commitment behind the words. The offer had been a gesture, not a contract.

So, Linda and I traveled through Taiwan, Hong Kong, Macau—gabbing the whole way, Linda studying her Japanese, both of us having the time of our lives. I was using my Peace Corps readjustment allowance, money intended to help me find a job back home. But none of us wanted to go home, let alone me. I'd send letters to my father, who'd put them in new envelopes and mail them from the States, so it looked like I'd returned. Then he'd forward the money. Half the Peace Corps volunteers I knew were doing the same thing.

When we were delayed, I sent Mr. Oku, my friend's father, a telegram: our flight would arrive at Osaka International Airport on such-and-such date, and I looked forward to meeting him.

He'd never heard of us. His son had never mentioned anything about two American women coming to live in his guest house. Mr. Oku received this telegram out of the blue from someone named Leslie, talking about flights and arrivals. He thought we were smugglers. He went to the Japanese equivalent of the FBI. They contacted Interpol, the American FBI, and investigated us thoroughly.

That's why we were the last people through customs at Osaka. They tore our luggage apart looking for contraband while Linda and I stood there, exuberant and oblivious, wondering what was taking so long.

But here's the remarkable thing: despite thinking we might be criminals, despite having every reason to refuse, Mr. Oku showed up at the airport with a sign that said, "Leslie and

Linda." His son had said he spoke English, but he didn't—not really. Still, he picked us up. He drove us to his home. The guest house was exactly as his son had described: an elevated structure with a little stream running alongside it. Exquisite.

I'd stumbled into that country through a cultural misunderstanding—an invitation that wasn't really an invitation, a telegram that triggered an international investigation—and stayed long enough to marry into it.

At my Shinto wedding reception a year later, I stood there in a kimono that had required some serious engineering. The silhouette runs straight down—no waist, no curves—because in Japan, the most erotic part of a woman's body is the nape of the neck, exposed by the deep dip at the back of the collar. The dressers had taken one look at me and produced cotton batting, packing it around my waist to build me out so my bust wouldn't break the line. (They had wanted to shave my face, too. There I drew the line.) There were many foreigners at the reception, and they started chanting: "Kiss the bride! Kiss the bride!" Toshi put his arm around my shoulder. We both looked at the camera and smiled. I love that photo. But the Japanese guests were offended. You do not touch in public. You do not smile at the camera. The bride is supposed to be demure, eyes downcast—not grinning like an American.

These were the lessons the State Department was trying to teach in a few weeks of training. I'd taken years to learn them, and I was still learning.

Every day, the training was somewhere different, something new. They taught us the cultural nuances: women don't shake hands with men. If an Iraqi man extends his hand, you put your hand on your chest, bow slightly, and greet him. Years later, I'd help train a Syrian refugee woman for her new job in America, and one of our role-playing exercises was exactly this—an American man puts out his hand, and you don't take it. Full circle.

I had a hell of a time just saying "*salaam alaikum*."

I returned to the lessons at hand. We studied Iraq's complex sectarian divisions, the lingering effects of the Iran-Iraq War, and the social disruption caused by the 2003 invasion. We learned about Sunni and Shia Islam, tribal structures, and the role of religious law in daily life.

The history was brutal and recent. Under Saddam Hussein, Iraq's Sunni minority had dominated the Shia majority for decades. The regime had crushed opposition with systematic violence: the 1982 massacre at Dujail, where nearly 150 Shia men and boys were killed after a failed assassination attempt; the Anfal campaign against the Kurds in the north, which killed tens of thousands; the brutal suppression of Shia revolts in 1991 and 1999. Saddam had been executed just five years earlier, in December 2006, but the wounds he'd inflicted were nowhere close to healed. The new government was dominated by Shia politicians, and Sunnis who had once held power now found themselves marginalized, suspected, and imprisoned. Deputy Prime Minister Mutlak, a Sunni Arab, had recently complained that at least ten thousand people—many from Sunni areas—had been held in jail for years without ever being brought to court. "We are not real partners in this government," he'd said. The sectarian math was simple and devastating: every policy decision, every appointment, every pardon carried the weight of generations of grievance.

We were being sent to help build a rule of law in a country where the law had been a weapon for so long that no one trusted it anymore. We needed to understand not just cultural differences, but how those differences had been weaponized during years of sectarian conflict. Why certain neighborhoods were off-limits to certain ethnic groups. How family connections could protect you or mark you for assassination. The way corruption worked within government institutions, and why direct confrontation often backfired whereas subtle relationship-building succeeded. Most importantly, we studied our own role in the broader mission.

As attorneys, we'd be spending more time in the Red Zone than almost anyone else at the embassy. While other personnel could conduct their work from the Embassy compound, we needed to visit prisons, law schools, courts, and government offices. Our job required regular exposure to the most dangerous environment in one of the world's most dangerous countries.

The reality of that danger was reinforced constantly. American and Iraqi officials were killed regularly. More than two hundred Iraqi civilians died every month from ongoing violence.

At the main embassy building, which I had yet to see save for the image flashed on the overhead screen, a huge copper plaque listed the names of all Americans killed in Iraq since the end of major combat operations. Not during the war, but during the so-called reconstruction period, when we'd be working. The message was clear: people were dying, and would continue dying, and we needed to be psychologically prepared for that reality.

***

The advanced tactical training, which overlapped the cultural training, took place in West Virginia at a facility that looked like a movie set. The level of investment was staggering—explosives demonstrations, elaborate driving courses, situational awareness exercises with professional actors. A car was detonated to show us what an IED explosion looked like.

The group heading to Iraq in that class represented a cross-section of federal service that surprised me. We had about thirty to forty people total: Justice Department attorneys like me, but also food service workers who'd be running embassy dining facilities, administrative staff from various agencies, communications specialists, and support personnel from virtually every federal department. Some people were heading to Iraq for three months, others for six months or a full year. Everyone needed the same basic preparation, regardless of their specific role.

What struck me immediately was the gender divide in rule-following. Before we'd even arrived in West Virginia, we'd received detailed instructions: buy motion sickness pills, bring anti-nausea spray, pack old clothes because training would be physically demanding. Every woman in the group followed these directions precisely. Not one of the men had bothered.

The pattern continued throughout the week. When instructors explained safety protocols for the driving course, women listened carefully and followed procedures exactly. Men assumed they could handle anything and often ignored guidelines they considered unnecessary. The result was predictable: by the second day, you could find men standing on grassy hillocks scattered around the professional racing course, having gotten sick from high-speed maneuvers in armored vehicles and needing to exit mid-exercise.

It wasn't just machismo, though that was part of it. The men seemed to operate on the assumption that rules were suggestions, that their individual judgment trumped institutional wisdom. Women, perhaps because we'd had to prove ourselves in professional environments where small mistakes could derail careers, understood that rules often existed for good reasons and that following them made everyone's experience more effective.

When I'd been asked to mark a security clearance box about past drug use, I'd agonized over two puffs of marijuana from my brother's hippie party twenty years earlier. Most people would have simply checked "no," but I couldn't. In any event, despite my admission, my top-secret security clearance was reinstated.

Years later, when I told my brother Dave about my conundrum, he said, "My God, Leslie, I don't remember you ever taking a hit. Why would you tell them you did?" Apparently, Dave was so high at his pig roast that he had no recollection of urging me to take a puff.

Toshi had never shared my reverence for rules. When we'd left Japan with Cary, then four months old, Japanese law limited each person to carrying four thousand dollars in currency—twelve thousand total for our family. Toshi's solution was to tape cash over his entire body. His torso, his legs, his arms—all wrapped in currency like some elaborate papier-mâché project, except the paper was money.

I was terrified. Not of getting caught, exactly, though that was part of it—I was terrified of the casual way he'd decided the rules simply didn't apply to him. This was a man who'd grown up in a mansion with servants. Rules had always been for other people to follow.

"I'm getting on that plane with the baby," I'd told him, "And I'm going to America." Whatever happened to him at customs was his problem. We made it through without incident, but I'd spent the entire time imagining Japanese officials unwrapping my husband like a mummy. He'd found the whole thing amusing. I'd found it representative of something fundamental between us.

My broader philosophy about rules was clear: I had great respect for the rule of law, even when individual laws seemed unjust or unnecessary. In a democracy and any free society, it cannot be up to individuals to pick and choose which laws to follow. The remedy is to take whatever action is necessary to change the law—through litigation, through legislatures, through proper channels. But until the law changes, it must be followed.

Take, for example, the Swine Flu case I refused to pursue. The case involved Mrs. Cordillo, a young woman who'd developed Guillain-Barré syndrome after receiving the swine flu vaccine. She was hospitalized at Yale New Haven, and although the majority of GBS patients recover, an accident with the respirator left her with catastrophic brain damage. Legally, causation was unprovable: her symptoms had appeared outside the six- to ten-week liability window the government recognized, and an intervening gastrointestinal illness could itself have triggered GBS. Over years of depositions and hearings, I got to know her husband, Charles, and I visited Mrs. Cordillo in the nursing facility where she'd lived since the accident. The judge awarded three million dollars anyway—the facts were simply too sympathetic.

Then Main Justice wanted to sue Yale New Haven Hospital, whose malfunctioning respirator had turned a recoverable case into a permanent vegetative state. Yale was negligent. They would have settled. But Connecticut law at that time prohibited contribution among tortfeasors. I told the U.S. Attorney I refused. It wasn't a moral objection—Yale was negligent. But I wasn't putting my name on a filing that the law didn't support. Another attorney handled it. Yale settled for one million dollars. That doesn't make it right. I wasn't into blind obedience. I'd maintained professional integrity throughout my career by refusing to compromise on positions I believed were legally unsound.

***

The driving course was particularly intense. We learned ramming techniques—how to hit another vehicle at maximum speed, preferably targeting the front axle rather than the back to disable their ability to pursue or prevent our escape. We practiced escape maneuvers, obstacle navigation, and situational assessment at highway speeds.

During one exercise, the instructor asked if anyone had experience with ramming. I was the only one who raised my hand, which shocked him. Here was a grandmother volunteering for a ramming experience.

"I didn't mean to do it," I explained, which got a laugh.

"That's not what ramming means in this course," he replied. "Here, ramming means hitting a car at maximum speed when enemies are blocking your escape route."

I should note that I am not a good driver.

The final exam was just me and an instructor in an armored vehicle, driving through scenarios designed to test threat recognition and decision-making under pressure. At one point, I saw a car stopped by the side of the road with a man and a woman standing beside it. The hood wasn't up, the trunk wasn't open—no obvious signs of mechanical trouble.

This immediately reminded me of something that had happened to a colleague during my earlier DOJ assignment in Bogotá, and how she'd learned threat detection the hard way. She'd arrived on an earlier flight and was picked up by what she thought was a standard government van. She sat in the front passenger seat, relaxed, probably thinking about the work ahead. Then motorcycles appeared behind them—policemen on bikes, red lights flashing, sirens wailing. The normal response to police signals: Pull over immediately. But the driver ignored them.She started to panic. "You have to pull over," she told him, her voice rising. "They're going to arrest us—stop the car!" The driver kept driving. She tried to open the window; it was locked. She reached for the door handle; it was also locked. That's when she realized she was sealed inside an armored vehicle. She couldn't get out even if she wanted to. She was waving frantically, trying to signal to the "policemen" that something was wrong, that she needed help.

"They're not cops," the driver said calmly, accelerating. "They're kidnappers." He gunned the engine and ran a red light with the fake police in pursuit.

The woman was hysterical by the time they reached our secure location. She wanted to turn around and go straight back to the airport. "Take me home. I don't want to be here."

I probably would have taken it in stride—I'd already learned that danger was often part of international work. But not everyone had developed that particular tolerance.

My analysis in this training situation was swift: this wasn't a breakdown. The car was positioned to create a roadblock, and the couple was there to make the scene look innocent. I executed a quick spin turn and took an alternate route up a hill.

At the top of the hill, the "enemy" was waiting. They opened fire with what felt like mortars, hitting the passenger side of our vehicle. I could see the flames, feel the impact, and hear the explosive sounds. The special glass held, but the realism was extraordinary.

I passed the test, but later learned I'd made the wrong decision. The couple had been innocent civilians, and my evasive action had led directly into the ambush I was trying to avoid. The lesson was sobering: in a war zone, threat assessment is incredibly difficult, and even experienced professionals regularly get it wrong. The difference between survival and disaster often comes down to split-second decisions based on incomplete information.

***

Another session covered contingency plans for worst-case scenarios: what to do if taken hostage, how to behave during interrogation, and the official protocols for different types of capture situations. I found myself preparing for possibilities that went beyond the official guidance. I drafted a speech in my head—what I would say if I were kidnapped and forced to make a propaganda recording. I wanted to be ready with words that would sound cooperative to my captors but signal to anyone who knew me that I was speaking under duress.

In Japan, a group of us foreigners had signed up with casting agencies for extra work in movies and television. We were just extras—background faces, nothing more. Airport scenes where we'd climb the boarding stairs and wave goodbye. Cocktail party scenes, which were the most fun because we all knew each other, and they served real alcohol even during dress rehearsals. By the final take, we'd be laughing and dancing, genuinely enjoying ourselves.

Then one day, they asked me to do a speaking part for NHK, the national broadcasting network. I said sure, no problem. It was in Japanese, but I could handle that. They dressed me in old-fashioned Japanese garb, put my hair up in a topknot, and placed me in a room full of Japanese men seated around a low table. I was serving them—a concubine, it turned out. And then they put the camera right in my face for a close-up. I froze. Completely froze. I was fine as an extra, having fun in the background, but with that camera inches away, I couldn't remember a single line. They kept having to cut my part shorter and shorter. It was a nightmare.

The show aired on NHK. My name was in the credits. I was teaching English at the YMCA at the time, and my students thought it was hilarious—their teacher, a concubine on national television.

That ended my acting career. But I filed the experience away—not the failure, but the claim.

During training, when we discussed what to do if captured and forced to make propaganda recordings, I knew exactly what I'd say: I had acting experience. I could read their script with great passion and credibility. Whether I'd actually perform under that pressure, with a camera in my face and my life on the line, I had no idea. I'd frozen playing a concubine on NHK. Would mortal fear focus me or shatter me completely?

More darkly, I accepted that if capture seemed inevitable and alternatives were exhausted, I would choose to end my own life rather than become a propaganda tool or intelligence asset for hostile forces. This wasn't a decision made lightly or from despair, but from a calculated assessment of what kinds of outcomes I could accept and which I could not.

***

My family remained puzzled by the entire enterprise, particularly Cary. "Mom, this seems so dangerous," he'd say, as if I'd never done anything risky before. I was patient with his worry, even slightly amused by his assumption that this represented some dramatic departure from my normal behavior. Cary's emotional sensitivity made him a wonderful son, but it also made it impossible for him to understand why I found uncertainty energizing rather than terrifying.

Maybe Cary couldn't understand what drove me because people who are motivated differently have a hard time imagining what motivates someone else. But it wasn't just that he didn't understand my reasons for going—it was that Iraq had become synonymous with danger in a way my other assignments hadn't.

He should have been used to this. He'd grown up watching me travel constantly. Every year, I went to Uganda, working for a nonprofit that ran an early childhood development center and a high school in the northern part of the country, right near the border where Joseph Kony and the Lord's Resistance Army operated. Northern Uganda in those years was a landscape of trauma. The LRA had terrorized the region for decades—a guerrilla group led by Kony, a former altar boy who'd dropped out of school at sixteen and now claimed to be visited by spirits, a spokesperson for God waging holy war. His forces had killed over one hundred thousand people, abducted sixty-six thousand children to serve as soldiers and sex slaves, and displaced two million from their homes. The government's response had been nearly as brutal—helicopter gunships burning villages, concentration camps where displaced families languished. Everyone knew the story of the Aboke Girls: in 1996, LRA rebels had demolished a wall at St. Mary's boarding school and taken 139 girls, ages thirteen to sixteen, into the bush. An Italian nun followed the trail of candy wrappers and plastic bottles the rebels had dropped after looting the school's Independence Day supplies. She brought money to buy the children back. Most eventually escaped or were released, but not all. One student leader who resisted was beaten, tied to a tree in the jungle, and left to die. The village where our school was located had experienced a major massacre. Maybe Cary didn't know all of that specific detail at the time. He just knew Mom went to Africa.

The compound where I stayed had no running water, no electricity. An enormous well dominated the courtyard, and these little kids had to pump water by hand—something we can't even imagine in this country, where authorities would never allow children to live without water and electricity. Every year, I had a different project. One year, I raised money for thirty sewing machines, school supplies, and clothing. Another year, I bought $2,000 worth of sporting equipment in the capital. There was even a multinational $400,000 grant to bring electricity not just to the school compound but to all the surrounding villages. I made four trips.

I stayed with the husband and wife who ran the school and became very close to them. Then we discovered they'd embezzled money from the grant. I never returned.

Cary had watched me bounce off to places like this for years—Uganda, Bosnia, the Philippines, Colombia. He'd grown up with a mother who disappeared for weeks or months to work in places most people couldn't find on a map.

But Iraq was different. Iraq was on the news every single night. Every news cycle showed violence, casualties, and

American soldiers dying. When I'd gone to Uganda or Bosnia or Bogotá, those places weren't dominating headlines. The danger existed, but it wasn't in everyone's face the way it was in Iraq. Cary wasn't just worried about his mother taking another international assignment. He was worried about his mother deploying to the most visible war zone in the world. That distinction mattered to him in ways I couldn't quite shift, no matter how many times I reminded him that danger had always been part of my work.

The truth was, I didn't expect anyone to die. Despite all the training in tourniquets and weapons and emergency procedures, despite the statistics about American casualties and the copper plaque in the embassy lobby, I approached the deployment with my characteristic confidence that preparation and competence would be sufficient protection. I wasn't afraid because I'd never learned to be afraid of professional challenges. Fear had simply never been part of my emotional vocabulary when it came to work that mattered.

The bulletproof vest and tourniquets were tools for survival. The real purpose was justice.

CHAPTER 4

INSIDE THE WIRE

They packed us in like cargo—roughly two hundred people strapped into web seats in the belly of a C-130, knees touching, no windows, no bathrooms, no conversation possible over the engine roar. We sat there in bulletproof vests and helmets for nearly two hours, and I watched the virtually expressionless faces around me—attorneys, State Department personnel, military contractors. Calm, determined, they all showed varying degrees of resignation to the conditions.

It had never occurred to me to ask: How do I actually get to Iraq?

I'd already shipped my supplies in advance—free of charge, with special postal stickers. I'd sent any number of boxes ahead: bedding, towels, blankets, and my computer. We had to bring everything we'd need for a full year. I didn't pack books—instead, I loaded 400 titles onto my Nook, a much smarter solution. All of this meant I could travel light.

While I hadn't expected no-frills military transport, I had expected privations once I arrived in Baghdad. That's why I'd taken care of myself first. Just ten days earlier, I'd been floating in the Dead Sea at the Mövenpick Resort in Jordan, indulging in three-hour massages with rock salt scrubs and mud wraps at the Evason Ma'in Hot Springs & Six Senses Spa. About $600 a day of pure luxury—a practical decision that would mystify my family but made complete sense to me. I knew that for the next twelve months, I wouldn't be getting massages, saunas, or any of the creature comforts I would have liked to become accustomed to. The spa had been exquisite, the ancient city of Petra breathtaking, the overnight Bedouin camp in the desert an adventure. I'd explored Wadi Rum, that spectacular protected wilderness with its mountain landscapes and ancient rock drawings, building monuments on sand dunes that the fine sand immediately swallowed.

If you're about to spend a year in what I thought would be Spartan conditions, under constant threat, why not prepare with the best possible relaxation?

Now, back in that cargo hold, the contrast was almost absurd. The person next to me kept shifting uncomfortably, trying to find space that simply didn't exist.

I'd pulled out my brand-new diplomatic passport at the Jordan airport—still crisp, unmarked by stamps, so different from the seven regular passports sitting in my desk drawer back home, thick with visas and entry stamps from all the countries I'd visited. There was my regular passport—first issued in 1965 for my Peace Corps travel to the Philippines—and the two official government ones from Justice attorney assignments, like that Ukraine case, where I'd interviewed witnesses in Moscow, Kyiv, and Transnistria. Each one told the story of a different version of myself—young idealist, seasoned attorney, international troubleshooter.

But this diplomatic passport was different. It meant I wasn't just traveling on government business—I was representing America itself, with all the protections and responsibilities that came with it. Yet here I was, strapped into a cargo plane like freight.

I suppose we'd all expected to get on an airplane—a real airplane, with seats and windows and maybe a meal service. Instead, we were human packages being delivered from point A to point B, strapped in so tight we couldn't move, reduced to the essential elements of what we were: bodies with specific skills, being transported to where those skills were needed.

With my background in law enforcement, I'd taken seminars on the importance of body language and facial expressions. I was pretty good at reading a room. Yet no one showed any emotion other than stoic acceptance.

If the transport was a shock, however, stepping off that plane in Baghdad was like entering a different universe entirely. The Baghdad Airport runway stretched endlessly under a harsh sun, the air shimmering with heat and dust that had a metallic taste. Armed soldiers moved with efficient precision, directing us toward massive, armored vehicles that looked more like tanks than buses; they were called "Rhinos." The convoy to the embassy compound took us through streets I couldn't see—the windows of our armored vehicle were too small, too thick, and too high. It felt as though we were viewing the world through a periscope. What I could glimpse looked like a city frozen in time, with blast walls and checkpoints creating a maze of concrete and steel.

This was my first glimpse of what would become routine: everything in Iraq was either heavily armored, heavily guarded, or both.

Then we passed through the first set of gates, and I got my first real look at Fortress America. The New Embassy Compound—everyone called it the NEC—sprawled across one hundred four acres like a small American city dropped into the heart of Baghdad. Sand-colored buildings rose four stories high, everything new and utilitarian, connected by paved walkways and surrounded by walls within walls within walls. T-walls—those eighteen-foot concrete barriers—created corridors and safe zones, while guard towers punctuated the perimeter like chess pieces. This was the most expensive U.S. embassy in the world, a $750 million fortress designed to house 1,400 Americans in complete isolation from the country they'd come to help rebuild.

Soldiers constantly patrolled the compound, and every entrance was heavily fortified and guarded. When demonstrations broke out, the compound went into lockdown. A perfect example? The Day of Rage, in which thousands of protesters gathered in Tahrir Square and across the country to demonstrate against corruption, high unemployment, and poor public services, resulting in violent clashes with security forces that left at least twenty-nine people dead. T-walls blocked all entrances. No one in, no one out.

But what struck me first were the palm trees: isolated, towering, scattered across the compound, with just a few pathetic leaves at the top, offering absolutely no shade. They looked rather silly standing there in the desert heat, and all I could think was, *How much money did we spend to have palm trees shipped to Iraq?* Because I already knew the cardinal rule: nothing, absolutely nothing, was ever purchased in Iraq. Not even water. Everything had to be imported in convoys, at enormous expense, for safety reasons.

Those palm trees were absurd—but they were also invisible money. Someone had signed the contracts, arranged the logistics, paid the bills, and there they stood as if they'd always been there. No price tags. No invoices fluttering in the wind. Just expensive objects existing without explanation.

It reminded me, oddly, of Toshi.

***

When I met Toshi, he wore Bally shoes, expensive tailored clothes, and a Rolex. But he'd been introduced to me as a chauffeur, so that's what I assumed he was.

My friend Giselle—a Parisian who was the companion of a wealthy Japanese man—had invited me to join them at an exclusive club. His chauffeur would pick us up, she'd explained. We arrived to find a room full of women who were drop-dead gorgeous and, I eventually understood, all hired for the evening. Giselle and I were the only ones who weren't.

Then the chauffeur walked in and sat down with us. *Strange*, I thought, *for a chauffeur to join the party*. But I didn't dwell on it.

After that evening, Toshi started coming to my apartment. His English was limited then, so he'd arrive with little handwritten notes. "Can I have a date with you?" "Can we go out?"

We started seeing each other, and over the weeks that followed, he took me to the finest restaurants, the best clubs, the most exclusive events in a city where everything was extraordinarily expensive. When I think back on how unobservant I was—I was simply enjoying the lifestyle without questioning any of it.

Once, leaving a restaurant with Giselle, she stopped at a display case near the door. Inside was an old earthenware mug, priced at $400. "Oh, Toshi," she said, "I really want this." He turned to the woman behind the counter: "Will you wrap it up and give it to her?" We walked out, wrapped mug in hand. As you do.

Eventually, he appeared with another note. "I love you madly. I cannot live without you. Will you marry me?"

I said yes. Why not? He was handsome, generous, and kind.

I insisted on a Shinto wedding—I wanted it authentically Japanese. If it didn't work out, I figured I'd just go back to America, and no one would ever know I was married. Two weeks before the ceremony, he presented me with a formal note, very proper. He was being disinherited for marrying me. The honorable thing was to call off the wedding.

I looked at this man I'd assumed was a chauffeur and said I wasn't canceling my wedding because he was getting disinherited. He was the one being disinherited? It did not make sense. I was having my wedding.

The ceremony cost a fortune—five hundred dollars just to rent the geisha, thirty thousand for the outer kimono. His family didn't attend. In Japan, inheritance works much like England: the eldest son takes everything, because land is too valuable to divide. Marry an unsuitable woman, and out you go.

What I only understood afterward was that Toshi hadn't been born into wealth at all. He'd been adopted into it. The family needed to continue a samurai lineage—twelve hundred years of it—and custom required bringing in the nearest male relative who wasn't a first son. That was Toshi. He'd grown up in a thirty-room mansion with a staff of servants, raised as the necessary heir rather than the natural one. Maybe that made it easier to walk away.

What I also learned after the wedding was that he'd never been a chauffeur. It had been his idea of a joke. Apparently, you haven't mastered a foreign language until you've mastered the humor.

***

My apartment was in SDA4—State Department Apartments—on the fourth floor, which turned out to be convenient for an unusual reason: it was designated as the "safe haven" where we'd assemble if the embassy walls were breached. The apartments had been designed as single-occupancy units and later divided: the bedrooms sat on the exterior of the building, with four-inch-thick windows facing outward; the kitchen and living room occupied the interior, with no windows at all. That was the architecture of safety—move inward, eliminate exposure entirely. The elevator lobby was stocked with pallets of MREs—Meals Ready to Eat—with a sign posted above: "The MREs are for emergency use only. RSO [Regional Security

Officer] permission required to access MREs." As if any of the residents would want to eat one under normal circumstances? But, yes, if we were attacked, for sure, we would have food.

Large pallets of water bottles were stacked in the elevator lobbies and along all the hallways. Medical supplies were strategically placed at building entrances—along with containers of antidotes we'd been trained to administer in case of chemical attack. At every entrance, there were canisters where you placed your weapon barrel while unloading it, in case of accidental discharge. Everything was designed with the possibility in mind that we might have to survive an attack.

Every Monday morning, they tested the warning systems. The sirens would sound, a drill would be announced, and we'd go through the motions.

From my bedroom window, which I'd been given a key for upon arrival, I could see two bunkers labeled 7K and 7L. When the sirens sounded—and they would sound with some frequency—announcing, "Incoming, incoming, get away from the windows, take cover, wait for the all clear"—we had five seconds to reach the nearest bunker. That voice making those announcements would become as familiar as family.

But the strangest part wasn't the security measures. It was the luxury existing alongside the constant sense of possible danger.

I called home to let my family know I'd made it safely. One unexpected benefit was having a DC telephone number that would allow our families to call us at no charge, and we could call anyone without paying either. After putting some of my belongings away, I strolled to the Dining Facility Air-

Conditioned (DFAC), which was unlike anything I'd ever experienced. At the center was a circular area devoted entirely to fruit from around the world, where staff would peel your quince, mango, or whatever exotic selection caught your eye. Then you walked along endless buffet lines featuring filet mignon every day, cuisine from dozens of countries, and an entire section devoted to ice cream. The person who sat beside me at my table mentioned that the Sunday-night lobster and prime rib dinners drew crowds like a cruise ship special event. Something to look forward to. Near the entrance, a single table was set but never occupied—a formal place setting in honor of military personnel still missing. It was easy to walk past without registering it. I didn't, after the first time.

The compound, as I explored it, seemed to have everything: two gyms, a Subway, a Green Bean coffee shop, and a Pizza Hut—windows, really, as opposed to sit-down restaurants—an indoor Olympic-sized swimming pool, a basketball court, a PX, laundry service, a barber shop, a U.S. Post Office, and a bank. There was even a bar named Baghdaddy's that, according to a sign, operated Thursday and Friday nights, where different embassy groups took turns providing bar service.

It was American consumer culture recreated inside a fortress—while outside the walls, explosions echoed through the streets of Baghdad.

The training in DC, not to mention the newspapers, taught me that people were being executed in front of their homes, and families were fleeing assassinations and bombings. Iraq was bleeding, trying to rebuild from decades of dictatorship and years of war. And here we were eating lobster and playing bartender with military money. We couldn't buy anything with our dollars, so this was how we were to buy extras.

The contrast, and I could feel it right from the beginning, felt like the burden I'd carried my whole adult life—the weight of unearned advantages. We didn't talk about it in those terms back when I was a kid, but I epitomize white privilege. I was born in America to an intact family, born healthy, born bright. Yes, my mother died when my siblings and I were young, but still—I'm a member of Mensa, and I didn't have to work for any of it. It just was what it was.

Maybe I connected with just how lucky I was and am during childhood. My stepsister Joanne arrived a year or so after my mother died, when my father married her mother. She was extremely lucky that my father came on the scene—though lucky hardly captures it.

Before us, Joanne had been living in Boston with an uncle's family in a tenement. The backyard wasn't grass. It was charcoal. Her troubled mother had put her on a train at five years old and sent her up there alone. Then my father came into her life, and everything changed. Suddenly, she had a nice house in West Hartford, vacations, skiing lessons, and good schools. A stable, loving parent. The same things I'd always had without thinking about them.

I didn't earn any of that. I just had it. Joanne showed me what it looked like to not have it—and what it meant when someone finally did.

The thing is, when you have gifts you didn't earn, you have a moral obligation to make use of them in a productive way. Not productive in terms of earning money—that was never a driver for me. Productive in terms of giving back. Again, that's what had driven me to the Peace Corps, to Bosnia, to the US Justice Department, to federal government service, now to Iraq. But sitting in an air-conditioned fortress with all amenities imaginable while Iraqis struggled, even died outside, made that responsibility feel both urgent and impossibly complicated.

Joanne had understood the gift because she'd lived without it. Toshi never had that reference point.

Toshi's relationship with money had been formed in a world I couldn't fully imagine, even after living in Japan. When he'd moved into my apartment in Japan, I came home one day to find a man surrounded by bolts of fabric. Toshi was having an entirely new wardrobe made.

"What are you doing?"

"I have to get a job," he said, as if this were obvious. "So, I have to get these new clothes."

He already had an unbelievable wardrobe. But in his mind, new circumstances required new clothes—dozens of them, custom-tailored. Come to think of it, he did get a job selling real estate without a license, and he was good at it. Handsome, personable, comfortable with wealthy clients. He had no particular skill for it, no training whatsoever. But all of his friends were multi-millionaires—that was his world. And in Japan, real estate deals involve no negotiation. None. If the price is five million, it's five million. You don't haggle. You don't counteroffer. You simply pay, or you don't. For someone with wealthy connections and no aptitude for negotiation, it was the perfect job. Land in Japan was extraordinarily expensive, and he made a lot of money. But the logic of money eluded him. When my father planned to visit us in Japan, I came home to find a blue car parked outside our apartment with our license plate on it.

"What did you do?"

"I had to buy a new car. Your father's coming."

"The old car was only nine months old."

"I don't want to embarrass you. We have to have a new car."

He'd never owned a car for more than a year, and bought two each year since he was fifteen—one Japanese, the other foreign. My father, a practical New Englander, couldn't have cared less what we drove.

This pattern followed us to America. After weeks of vacation—Hawaii, Las Vegas, San Francisco, six weeks in Miami—we arrived in Connecticut and moved in with my father. Toshi went to buy a car and came back with a yellow Mustang. A two-seater with no backseat. We had a four-month-old baby. I was pregnant again, courtesy of Hawaii.

"Toshi," my father said, with the patience of someone explaining gravity, "you don't pay cash for a car like that. You finance it and pay it off. You need to build credit in America."

The concept was foreign to him—not the words, but the underlying reality. Why would you need to prove you could pay for things? You simply paid for them. He exchanged the Mustang for a Grand Prix, but I don't think he ever understood what my father was trying to teach him. Toshi had lived in a bubble—servants, wealth, complete insulation from ordinary concerns. He'd simply never had to reckon with the gap between his reality and everyone else's.

Watching Americans at the embassy compound, I wondered how many of us would leave Iraq having never really understood what life here was actually like. And I wondered why I could see it when others couldn't.

In the Philippines, the country had asked the U.S. to send volunteers. They identified their needs—education, agriculture, sanitation—and requested help addressing the serious issues they recognized. We lived in villages, ate local food, learned the language, taught in their schools. We saw their reality because we were inside it.

Iraq hadn't invited us to build an eight-billion-dollar fortress where Americans lived in complete comfort with every amenity provided free. The Peace Corps model was about accepting an invitation and working alongside people who wanted assistance. This felt like imposing ourselves on a country with the message "you need us," whether they agreed or not. The war was over. We could have just left. Instead, we'd created this expensive, insulated American enclave and called it reconstruction.

Glancing outside the window, I spotted a huge thermometer on the side of one embassy building. I quickly learned that temperatures of 110 and 120 weren't unusual at all, even though I'd arrived in February. One day, it would hit 130 degrees.

***

The embassy compound was where I lived, but it wasn't where I'd work. For the foreseeable future, I'd be stationed at FOB Prosperity—the Forward Operating Base and Army base—built on the grounds of one of Saddam Hussein's palaces.Still inside the wire. Just a different section of it.

The Green Zone connected everything—embassy, FOB, the International Zone where Iraqi government buildings stood behind their own blast walls.

Every morning, my new colleague and I would grab keys from a basket in the carpool area, find the corresponding vehicle in a lot full of them, and drive ourselves through the Zone to Saddam's former stables. As long as we stayed inside the wire, we had complete autonomy. We could move freely within the American-controlled bubble, which felt almost like normal life if you didn't think too hard about what lay beyond the T-walls.

FOB Prosperity was a different world from the embassy—less polished, more operational—but it was still Fortress America.The building where our Provincial Reconstruction Team (PRT) worked was a long, single-story brick structure that had been renovated but retained its original character as Saddam Hussein's horse quarters. Saddam's palace, while extensively damaged by US missiles, housed a gym and other facilities regularly used by military and embassy personnel.

There were many other buildings as well as a pool and bathhouse on the grounds, and scattered throughout the palace complex were palace furnishings, including the ornate chairs where Saddam had once held court—massive, elaborate thrones designed to intimidate anyone who approached them. Near the DFAC, a row of small Iraqi-owned shops sold rugs and everyday goods—a strip of civilian commerce tucked inside a military compound, as ordinary as it was incongruous. A decorative pool was an added touch. Saddam had thirty-seven palaces scattered across Iraq. The same dinner was prepared in every single one, every evening. That way, no one would know which one to poison.

I took a photo of myself sitting in one of those chairs, finding dark humor in the irony: an American prosecutor dispensing justice from a dictator's former seat of power. I took another photo of myself standing in front of the door to Saddam's stable in full gear—helmet, forty-pound PPE (personal protective equipment), shrapnel-resistant goggles, a black tourniquet, a Leatherman knife, and a flashlight hanging from my vest, Nomex gloves—pointing at the building that now housed American democracy-building efforts.

The Provincial Reconstruction Team (PRT) was utilitarian—desks, chairs, basic equipment. From my window, three feet of air separated me from an eighteen-foot T-wall. A cross-shaped rack beside my desk held my PPE and helmet when they weren't on my body; the Kevlar plates had to be stored upright to prevent warping. But what struck me most was the freedom I had once I settled in. This wasn't like my structured role as a Justice Department trial attorney in DC. Here, I could essentially design my own mission. There was a director who'd been there a couple of years and knew the terrain, but the approach was remarkably informal. He'd take new arrivals around: "Let's visit this law school, this prison, this juvenile detention facility." You'd see what was available, what needed attention, and then you'd volunteer for whatever projects interested you.

Each of the ten attorneys just did whatever we wanted. You'd carve out your focus—"I want to do this"—and nobody cared. No one was asking, "Leslie, what are you doing today?" It was like being turned loose in a democracy laboratory, free to experiment with whatever caught your attention.

I loved this kind of freedom; I was born for it. After thirty-two years of being handed case assignments, Iraq finally let me operate the way my father had taught me to think.

I got in trouble constantly with the nuns, mostly for talking. When I stood in the hallway at St. Joseph's Cathedral for talking in class—kids would walk by on their way to lunch and say, "Hey Lee, what's going on?" and then I'd have to answer and stay even longer. My father just shrugged when I told him about it. One time, a group of us were riding the public bus home in our uniforms, elementary school girls, and we started singing. Someone reported us to the principal. We had to write one hundred times: I will not sing on the bus. My father thought it was a joke. What kind of people take offense at schoolgirls singing? His attitude was simple: the rule is stupid, but you play the game.

In ninth grade, my best friend and I skipped school entirely. We pooled our money, walked to the train station, and asked the ticket agent to send us as far as we could go and return on what we had. We ended up at some shore town—had lunch, went to the library, bought postcards, addressed them to the nuns, and mailed them. My father thought it was hilarious. We were top students. It was a lark.

He confirmed what I already suspected: some things are just stupid, and noticing that doesn't make you a bad person.

I found myself drawn immediately to the law schools. Baghdad had two—the University of Baghdad and Al-Nahrain

University—and I was interested in how law was taught and how it functioned in a post-dictatorship society. I was also interested in the juvenile detention system, which would become one of my major projects. The children in the system had caught my attention back in the States. Many as young as eight were being prosecuted for terrorism, often for simply carrying munitions that adults had ordered them to transport, and for sex-related crimes. They had no legal representation, no understanding of their rights, no advocate of any kind. The concept of children's rights was completely foreign in a legal system that had functioned under a dictatorship for decades. While the parents of the children implicit in the crimes had the right to have an attorney, the children did not. I could visit prisons, teach constitutional law concepts to guards and administrators. I could work with UN components and NGOs, which often hosted meetings at the embassy DFAC because everyone wanted an excuse to eat there. The freedom was intoxicating: if I met someone interesting, if I found a problem to solve, if I saw an opportunity to make an impact—I could pursue it.

The only real constraint was security. Every trip outside the Green Zone required a four-vehicle armored convoy, and we were always referred to as "packages" being transported from point A to point B. A maximum of four people per mission, but one spot was usually reserved for the interpreter, so it was usually just two or three of us and our translator, surrounded by fourteen armed guards. In vehicle two or three sat Diplomatic Security personnel. Through the darkened windows, we could see Iraqis going about their daily business.

***

On my second day of official duty, I went on my first mission to a law school. But before we even left, I got a thorough education in just what these missions actually entailed.

The head of our security detail was a young Black man—absolutely charming, professional, someone I would come to know well over the months. Before we entered the vehicles, he made sure we had our equipment on correctly, then gave us the same lecture we'd hear a hundred times, but which protocol demanded we hear every single time: "You cannot release your seat belts unless we order you to. You cannot move. You cannot do anything in the vehicle without permission. We're going to switch up which vehicle you're in—sometimes two, sometimes three—so the enemy doesn't know your pattern. But they'll know you're in two or three because the last vehicle is always different."

The last vehicle was unmistakable—it had a big hole in the back with a gun protruding from it. Which vehicle depended on who was running the mission. When State Department diplomatic security was responsible for our movements, we traveled in armored Suburbans. When the military moved us, we went in MRAPs—Mine-Resistant Ambush Protected vehicles that cost $5 million each—or in Humvee convoys. The MRAP had a device at the front that would explode bombs before we reached them. We sat strapped in the belly of this enormous vehicle, unable to see much of anything. If there was a roadblock or security issue, the driver crossed over the divided highway, smashing trees and plants in the median, because when there's a security concern, nothing else matters.

Above us, always, were four helicopters. From the other vehicles, you could see them clearly—four soldiers in each helicopter, two on each side, sitting in nets with their legs hanging out, flapping in the wind, massive guns pointed down at the streets below. And above the helicopters, drones were sending photographs and information back to command. Everything about our movements was classified—the type of convoy, the time we were leaving, the exact route. It was considered highly classified information.

Once we finally arrived at the law school, we waded past students walking around with piles of books, chatting, and pushing bikes. Most of the women wore headscarves—some the two-piece version that completely covered the hairline, others more loosely draped, stylish, and color-coordinated. In the 1960s, Iraqi women wore short skirts and blouses with low necklines. Before 2003, many chose not to cover their heads at all. But after the invasion, women started wearing scarves for protection—not devotion. Even Christian women who'd never covered for religious reasons began wearing them to avoid being singled out, followed, kidnapped, or shot. The headscarf had become a survival accessory.

The advance team had already swept the entire building with dogs. Snipers were positioned on the roof. Once inside the building, we could remove our helmets, but our vests had to stay on. We had to walk into the meeting room still wearing full protective gear, then we could finally remove the vests—but they had to be placed immediately behind our chairs with our helmets, within instant reach.

And there was a code word. "Get coffee," or whatever phrase they'd chosen that day. That was the signal: stop whatever you're doing, put on your helmet and vest, and leave immediately. No questions, no delays.

We arrived at the law school meeting where easily twenty Iraqi law professors had been waiting for hours with food laid out, having no idea when we'd show up because, again, our timing was classified. We walked in wearing all this gear, snipers on their roof, helicopters hovering overhead, armed guards throughout their campus. Our hosts sitting around a table in their own country, at their own law school, waiting to discuss legal reform with Americans who'd arrived like an invading army. Which made arriving at the law schools particularly awkward. It was their country. They were lawyers. This was a law school, a place dedicated to the rule of law. And we were like invaders. The power dynamic was terrible. I would feel it every single time.

We asked them what we could do, what they needed by way of books or lectures. I had lectured on the Constitution, and when they found this out, they said, "Oh, you lecture. Give us lectures on the Constitution."

On the way back to the embassy, our convoy was stopped by Iraqi police. The first vehicle had gotten through the intersection, but ours—the second in line—was detained. The lead vehicle immediately backed up, and two armed men from the vehicle behind us confronted the police until they backed off. For a newcomer, it was "exciting," as I wrote to my family, though that was a typical understatement. While it was concerning, it was also exhilarating and completely surreal:

American legal advisors driving through Baghdad in armored vehicles to meet with Iraqi law school faculty members to discuss legal issues confronting Iraq.

I remembered the psychiatrist's final assessment back in the States, how she'd dismissed me after I'd rattled off my credentials. I understood: they weren't just hiring lawyers. They were hiring lawyers who could stay focused on their mission under difficult and significant pressure in a war-torn country.

This was exactly the kind of scenario they'd tried to prepare us for during those days of training in D.C. and West Virginia—the unexpected confrontations, the split-second decisions, the need to stay calm when everything could go sideways in an instant. All those medical training sessions, the tourniquets and emergency procedures, to ensure we could function under pressure—it all made sense.

I found myself missing something I'd taken for granted in every other country I'd visited: the ability to wander through local markets, bargain for souvenirs, sit in cafes, and observe daily life. In the Philippines, Japan, Bosnia—everywhere I'd worked or visited—I could immerse myself in local culture. Here, I was hermetically sealed inside American infrastructure, observing Iraq only through bulletproof glass and carefully controlled meetings.

***

The yellow duck souvenirs I soon sent home probably captured the essence of our situation better than any formal report.

The PX sold little yellow rubber ducks that, when squeezed, played the exact same announcement we heard during mortar attacks: "Incoming, incoming. Get away from the windows. Take cover. Wait for the all clear." The voice was identical—the same matter-of-fact tone that could wake you from sleep and send you to the apartment's living room, which had no windows for shelter. I bought a dozen of them, thinking they were hilarious. Duck and cover—it was like those childhood nuclear attack drills in the fifties and sixties, except this was real.

I sent them home to my family, imagining their amusement when they heard that familiar voice coming from a bath toy. My sister Marilyn's response was typical. "That wasn't really funny. It wasn't funny at all. You think it's a joke?" She couldn't understand how I found humor in sounds that represented genuine danger, moments when mortars could actually crash down and kill people. To her, I was putting myself in unnecessary danger again, just like I always had.

After a few weeks of jumping out of bed every time the sirens sounded, racing from our bedrooms with their four-inch-thick windows—windows that could not be opened or penetrated by bullets or mortars—to the windowless living areas, my housemate and I stopped bothering. We'd hear "Incoming, incoming" and think, "I'm not getting out of bed for this." It wasn't bravado or recklessness—it was psychological adaptation. I felt safe. I only felt safe because the government knew it was unsafe.

Sometimes I'd look out into the embassy compound after the siren had gone off. There sat a heliport and a drone field where unmanned aircraft took off throughout the day, sometimes successfully, sometimes crashing in ways that reminded you this was still experimental technology in an active war zone. Crash, and get on with it.

I'd volunteered for the Trauma Responder Team—monthly training sessions on Fridays, our day off. Patient assessment. Triage. The categories we'd assign in a mass casualty: green for minor injuries, yellow for delayed, red for immediate, black for dead or "nonsalvageable." The goal was simple and brutal: do the greatest good for the greatest number.

During IV training, team members had to practice sticking each other. Some walked around with bruises at the entry sites for days. The instructors weren't interested in squeamishness.

Out in that compound, we trained with fake blood and elaborate wound scenarios. During one exercise, I volunteered to play a casualty with arterial bleeding from an upper arm wound. The fake blood came in a small pouch with a pump that I could squeeze to create realistic spurting. They gave me a bone protruding from my shoulder—all theatrical effects designed to prepare medics for the visual shock of real trauma. I was categorized as a level 4 casualty, critical condition, which meant I'd be evacuated by helicopter.

Except my pump malfunctioned. The blood wasn't flowing properly, so a medic reassessed me on the spot. "You're not really category four. You're three. Get up and walk to the nearest clinic for pain medication." I never got my helicopter ride.

But I got the photograph—sitting in a chair with the bone dramatically protruding from my bloodied shoulder. When I posted it, several relatives panicked. They'd seen the wound before reading the explanation and assumed the worst.

The fact that people who knew me well could mistake training for reality demonstrated exactly what the exercise was designed to address. In actual emergencies, visual information can be overwhelming and misleading. Training helped us process shocking scenes methodically rather than emotionally.

My family's horrified reaction to that photo—and to the yellow ducks—revealed something fundamental about how differently we processed danger. They saw threats I should avoid; I saw realities I needed to manage. I'd understood that distinction for a long time—longer than Iraq, longer than the law. It went back to something I'd learned young, before I had words for it.

My mother was here one day, gone the next, never discussed afterward as if she'd never existed. That taught me something stark about mortality: death comes whether you're ready or not, whether you've acknowledged it or not. The question isn't whether you'll die, but whether you'll have lived meaningfully before you do.

I'd told my sons once how I wanted to go out: giving a brilliant, impassioned speech in the well of a courtroom, then dropping dead from a brain aneurysm or heart attack. Out like a light, still wearing my boots and spurs, doing what I loved until the very last moment. They were horrified. But to me, it made perfect sense. My mother's death had been so abrupt, so unprocessed, leaving nothing but a rose-colored satin bathrobe and a jar of sour balls on a workbench as evidence she'd existed at all. If I were going to die—and everyone does—I wanted it to matter. I wanted to die in the middle of work that mattered, not fading away in some hospital bed, uselessly consuming resources.

Despite my take on my mother, or because of it—who knows?—I'm very optimistic. I always think everything is going to work out just great for me. And everything has.

CHAPTER 5

THE PRT DREAM

Agriculture specialists sat near State Department diplomats, military personnel worked alongside legal advisors, and development experts collaborated with translators. At the PRT, we could see what everyone else was working on, overhear their phone calls, and watch projects take shape across multiple areas of expertise.

It was the interdisciplinary collaboration I found so compelling about the PRT concept—all these different government agencies finally working together under one roof, rather than operating in their usual silos. The Department of Agriculture had its mission, the Department of Transportation had its, State Department personnel pursued diplomatic goals, and Justice Department attorneys like me focused on the rule of law. But we could participate in each other's projects when it made sense, when our expertise overlapped, and when an initiative needed multiple perspectives.

This was the model that had made sense to me from the beginning: looking at the whole picture, involving all parties with an interest, and addressing complex problems with comprehensive solutions. It was the Responsibility to Protect doctrine made real—not just military force, but reconstruction, legal reform, and humanitarian aid. Intervention reimagined as a partnership. And some days, it actually delivered.

The wheelchair distribution day was one of those days.

I first learned about it through the agriculture people at the PRT, who'd been coordinating with a nonprofit called Wheelchairs for Iraqi Kids. The founder was a CNN Hero of the Year—someone who'd made it his mission to collect, refurbish, and transport wheelchairs to children who'd never had access to basic mobility devices. When the Air Force agreed to transport more than a hundred wheelchairs from California to Iraq on a cargo plane, the PRT helped organize the distribution.

They chose a compound—located in what I thought might be a religious complex—and cordoned it off completely. Military vehicles surrounded the perimeter, and armed soldiers were positioned at every entrance. The security was absolute: nothing could happen to these children, not here, not during an American humanitarian operation.

Parents began arriving with their children, some from Baghdad, others from outlying provinces. I never learned how word had spread, what mechanism brought them there, but they came. Children with disabilities from birth defects, from accidents, and from IEDs. Children who'd spent their entire lives unable to move independently, carried everywhere they needed to go, entirely dependent on others for every change of position.

Leaning against the courtyard wall, I watched military personnel who'd received specialized training in wheelchair fitting—something I'd never even considered necessary. I'd assumed you just placed someone in a wheelchair, fastened the seatbelt, and sent them on their way. But they explained that you had to understand each child's weight, height, specific disabilities, and capabilities. Could they push themselves? Would they always need someone to wheel them? Did they have upper-body strength or control? Each wheelchair had to be precisely fitted, properly adjusted, and individually configured.

I stood there taking photographs, bearing witness as an observer rather than a participant. I hadn't received the training; my role was simply to be present, hand out candy and other treats to the children, and see American idealism in action.

Then they brought out an eight-year-old boy who'd never been in a sitting position in his life. His parents carried him, and I could see other siblings gathered around, watching. The military personnel carefully, methodically strapped him into the wheelchair, explaining each adjustment as they made it. The boy looked bewildered—this vertical world was entirely new to him. He'd spent eight years seeing the world from floor level, always horizontal, never upright.

A soldier knelt beside him, placed the boy's hands on the controls, and guided his fingers. "Just push this button," the soldier said through a translator. "Just push."

The wheelchair moved.

The look on that child's face—wonder doesn't capture it. It was like witnessing someone discover they had wings. He was moving himself, controlling his own direction for the first time in his life. The chair had a tray in front where he could eat, where he could place things, and where he could exist as a person at a table rather than a body on the floor.

His parents stood watching; other children pressed close. Someone brought stuffed animals, which we distributed to the kids. Someone else had snacks and drinks. These hardened military personnel—men and women trained for combat, carrying weapons, positioned here to protect against any threat—were in tears, hugging children, celebrating mobility as the miracle it was.

I felt it too, that validation of belief. It was exactly the kind of project I would have wanted to dream up myself—not just participate in but conceive.

I'd spent my adult life being drawn to exactly this kind of work, though I couldn't have articulated why until much later. Even as a teenager in Connecticut, I'd joined "Teens Against Polio," which organized fundraisers and awareness campaigns before most of my classmates knew what activism meant. It wasn't political—it was practical. People needed help. We had resources. The equation seemed simple.

Then John F. Kennedy launched the Peace Corps in 1961, the year I graduated from St. Thomas Aquinas High School, and suddenly that impulse had a name, a framework, a call to action that resonated with everything I felt but hadn't yet expressed. "Ask not what your country can do for you—ask what you can do for your country." It wasn't just rhetoric for me; it was permission.

Forty years later, here I was in Baghdad, still following that same compass. Still believing that American resources and expertise, applied thoughtfully and collaboratively, could help societies rebuild after devastation. The PRT model embodied everything I'd always believed intervention should look like.

This was what America should be doing in Iraq: not imposing democracy from above, but identifying needs, mobilizing resources, and solving problems that Iraqis couldn't solve on their own. Winning hearts and minds not through force but through tangible improvement in people's lives.

It was visible in a way that most interventions aren't. You can ship medications, but you can't photograph the moment a fever breaks. You can fund infrastructure, but it might take years before anyone sees results. But wheelchairs—wheelchairs transform lives immediately. Before and after. Immobile and mobile. Floor and eye level. Dependent and independent.

The photo opportunity wasn't lost on anyone. Military photographers documented everything, and everyone else was taking pictures too. This was the kind of story that needed to be told, the kind of American generosity that deserved recognition. Some cynics might call it propaganda, but standing there watching that eight-year-old boy move himself in circles, testing his new ability with increasing confidence, I didn't care about the optics. It was real. The transformation was real. American resources had created this moment, and that mattered.

This opposed to projects that sounded brilliant on paper but missed the mark entirely.

I'd heard about those, too, through the agriculture specialists who worked in the rambling stable-office alongside me. They'd been trying to improve Iraq's agricultural output, strengthen food security, and help farmers increase productivity. Noble goals, practical objectives. Someone had decided to build a huge facility to raise chickens, produce eggs, and process the meat—a comprehensive agricultural project that would employ Iraqis and feed communities.

The facility cost millions of dollars. It was professionally designed, properly constructed, and fully equipped. It represented exactly the kind of infrastructure development intended to demonstrate American commitment to Iraqi economic recovery.

There was just one problem: nobody had bothered to ask Iraqis if they actually wanted fresh local chicken. They didn't. They wanted frozen chicken from America—Purdue, specifically. The expensive facility sat largely unused, a monument to the assumption that our way was the best way, that what worked in America must work everywhere, that we didn't need to ask what people actually needed because obviously they needed what we were offering.

Even more absurd was the amusement park proposal. USAID had planned to build an entertainment complex on the banks of the Tigris River—rides, attractions, and a public gathering space for Iraqi families. Millions of dollars for Iraqi children to have fun, to experience normalcy, to enjoy childhood despite the ongoing violence.

Fortunately, that one never got off the ground. Everyone eventually recognized what should have been obvious from the start: what parent would take their child to a highly visible public amusement park in Baghdad? You might as well paint a target on your back. Why are you gathering in this Western, capitalistic venue? Why are you exposing your family to potential attack?

The same Americans who lived behind eighteen-foot T-walls, who traveled only in armored convoys, who checked vehicles with explosive-detecting dogs, who maintained constant armed security—those same Americans thought Iraqi families would casually spend an afternoon on carnival rides beside the river.

The wheelchairs were different. They came from America, yes, but they addressed a need that Iraqis had identified for themselves. They required no special infrastructure, no maintenance contracts, no ongoing American involvement. They simply gave children mobility, and that gift transcended cultural differences.

I thought about Japan. Yes, America had occupied Japan after World War II—there was no denying that fact. But MacArthur's administration had shown how occupation could become something more. What fascinated me was how they'd prepared. Before the occupation even began, the government had commissioned Ruth Benedict, an anthropologist who'd never been to Japan, to study everything about Japanese culture and psychology. She wrote *The Chrysanthemum and the Sword,* and her analysis became the blueprint for occupation policy. When officials wanted to prosecute the Emperor as a war criminal, Benedict explained why that would be catastrophic—she understood his symbolic position in Japanese culture. The Emperor wasn't touched. They made mistakes—briefly banning Kanji, then reversing course when they understood the damage. But they learned. American soldiers walked through Tokyo, handing out chocolate bars to children. In six years of occupation, not a single American soldier was killed by Japanese resistance. It became one of the most peaceful transitions of power in modern history.

What struck me was that America had done the right thing back then: understanding what they were getting into before they got into it. Learning first. Then acting. But we hadn't prepared for Iraq the way MacArthur had. Civil Affairs officers trained for Europe and Latin America were deployed with no introduction to Arabic or the Middle East. We were learning as we went, which meant making mistakes we might have avoided. And preparation wasn't even the deepest problem—legitimacy was. Iraq felt different. We hadn't exactly won a war—we'd toppled a government. We hadn't earned reconstruction rights through a decade of conflict that ended in unconditional surrender—we'd taken them through shock and awe. I wanted to believe the PRT model could bridge that gap, that thoughtful partnership could substitute for the legitimacy Japan had provided.

Working at FOB Prosperity meant I could observe these contrasts daily. I'd see agriculture specialists struggle with the disconnect between American farming methods and Iraqi realities. I'd watch State Department personnel try to navigate Iraqi political dynamics they barely understood. I'd participate in legal reform initiatives that assumed Iraqi courts would function like American courts if we just explained the right principles clearly enough.

But I also saw genuine collaboration. I watched military medics work alongside Iraqi doctors, each learning from the other. I saw development specialists genuinely listen to Iraqi community leaders before designing projects. I participated in meetings where Iraqis challenged American assumptions and Americans actually adjusted their approaches.

Sarah Ali, the Iraqi cardiothoracic surgeon I'd met during my first weeks, embodied that collaboration. This was the most meaningful relationship I had yet to form—perhaps one of only a few in the country. She was brilliant, articulate, and passionate about her work, with medical training that rivaled that of any American doctor. She worked part-time with our Provincial Reconstruction Team, one of the brave Iraqis who risked everything to collaborate with Americans. Like all Iraqi staff, she used a fake name.

During our training at the State Department in Washington, D.C., we learned that the instructor handling language, Iraqi history, and cultural training had been a State Department interpreter in Iraq. He was very good-looking, very well dressed, and very articulate. Someone in class asked him, "How'd you get here?"

He told us the story. Thirty Iraqi interpreters had their real identities exposed when a laptop was stolen—names, home addresses, families. Two were executed in front of their homes before the others could be evacuated. He was one of the thirty. His parents still believed he was living and studying in South America. They don't even know he was in the U.S.—they could still be in danger if anyone found out.

Before 2003, Iraq was known for its healthcare, which was technologically more advanced than that of most Middle Eastern countries. Students from across the region had flocked to Baghdad's universities. Now, more than five hundred of Iraq's leading medical professionals had been assassinated. Seven thousand more had fled the country after receiving death threats. Academics were being killed at a rate of more than one per week. In late March, Mohammed Alwan—a prominent Baghdad surgeon and dean of the medical faculty at al-Mustansiriya University—had been assassinated. He had no known political affiliations. A government that cannot protect its people, one Iraqi scientist said, does not deserve to be a government.

Sarah stayed anyway. She changed her clothing while en route to the PRT; she continued working with us, driven by something I deeply admired.

Working with Sarah and other Iraqis highlighted the contradictions of our mission. We had genuine relationships, real friendships that crossed cultural and political divides. I never directly asked Sarah why she took the risk, why she was willing to tell her family she did something else entirely. The question felt too dangerous, too likely to force her into articulating something better left unspoken. But I watched her work, saw her dedication, and recognized in her the same impulse that had driven me: the belief that service matters, that your expertise creates obligation, and that you do not turn away from people who need what you can provide.

We had lunch together in the dining facility at FOB Prosperity, less elaborate than the NEC but still serving food no Iraqi outside the Green Zone could readily access. We discussed our projects, shared frustrations, and compared notes on Iraqi bureaucracy versus American bureaucracy. The conversations remained carefully professional, focused on work rather than personal circumstances, but friendship existed in the spaces between our words.

I thought about her during the wheelchair distribution, wondered if she'd heard about it, and imagined what she'd think of American military personnel weeping over Iraqi children's joy. The PRT dream was supposed to be about exactly this kind of convergence: Americans and Iraqis working together toward shared goals, each contributing what they could, both sides benefiting from the collaboration. Some days it actually worked.

But even on the days when it worked, even when I watched an eight-year-old boy discover mobility, even when I saw soldiers and parents united in celebration of a child's transformation, I couldn't quite escape the fundamental contradiction we all lived with—and neither could the Iraqis watching us.

***

On the eighth anniversary of the American invasion—April 9, 2011—the protests shifted. Iraqis called it the Day of Salvation. Earlier demonstrations, including the Day of Rage, had targeted government corruption, lack of services, and abuses in the prisons. Now the sit-ins named the U.S. occupation itself as the central problem. Among those leading the crowds was Uday al-Zaidi, the brother of Muntazer al-Zaidi, the journalist who'd thrown his shoe at President Bush in December 2008. That moment had made him a hero to millions of Iraqis. Now his brother was organizing tents in front of American military bases, demanding our departure.

When the demonstrations swelled, the compound went into lockdown. I'd planned to spend the day sightseeing in the Green Zone with friends. Instead, T-walls blocked all entrances. No one in, no one out. We sat in our apartments watching news coverage of Iraqis demanding that we leave—coverage we could see but streets we couldn't reach. That same weekend, Americans in New York and San Francisco were marching against the same war.

But in those early months, working at Saddam's former stables alongside people from all those different agencies and backgrounds, I had the privilege of seeing that ideal in action. I had the privilege of believing it could work.

CHAPTER 6

ON PAPER

There was only one police college for the entire country—every single police officer received their education there. When I arrived to lecture, I faced a sea of men in uniform, hundreds of them filling the auditorium, so many that they looked like a single entity rather than individual people. The military discipline was palpable: backs straight, attention focused, no cross-talking. Their superiors watched from the sides, which probably helped enforce the discipline, but the atmosphere reminded me of West Point rather than a civilian police academy.

Under Saddam, police officers had been used as soldier substitutes. The notion of a good police officer was someone who relied on physical power. Now we were trying to teach something different: that a great policeman uses his brain rather than his fists. Gathering information from all sources. Thinking analytically. Using powers of observation. The shift from enforcer to investigator, from intimidation to evidence.

It was working, at least in the classroom. Officers and students were treated with respect and dignity—a direct result of human rights training and Iraq's new democratic ideals.

Whether any of it would survive contact with the streets was another question.

I'd been asked to lecture on the Constitution—and this is where the irony deepened. The Iraqi Constitution had been developed with the advice of constitutional scholars from multiple nations, including the U.S. The result was, in many ways, a masterpiece. It included explicit protections that our own Constitution lacks: the right to a clean environment, comprehensive healthcare rights, women's rights articulated in specific detail, protections for people with disabilities, extensive medical rights, and clear guidelines for juvenile justice. It was, frankly, the paradigm of a progressive constitution—at least on paper.

When I lectured on it, I found myself in a strange position, explaining the limitations of our own constitutional framework. "Our Constitution was written over two hundred years ago by farmers," I told the police officers. "It was created for an agrarian world that no longer exists. Yes, we've amended it over the decades. Yes, courts have interpreted provisions in evolving ways. But we're still fundamentally interpreting a document written 250 years ago, trying to apply eighteenth-century language to twenty-first-century problems."

I could see them processing this, trying to reconcile the image of American constitutional perfection with the reality I was describing. "There are constitutional issues that will reach our Supreme Court with this administration," I continued, "and the justices will be interpreting something written by men who couldn't have imagined the internet, or modern medicine, or the technology shaping our current lives."

"Your Constitution," I said, gesturing to include everyone in the room, "actually captures more modern rights directly. The challenge isn't the words on the paper. The challenge is enforcement, infrastructure, and the enormous distance between legal principles and lived reality."

The Iraqi Constitution was more progressive than ours in many respects. But enforcement required functioning institutions, trained personnel, cultural shifts, and political will—none of which could be conjured simply by drafting beautiful constitutional language. Federal laws, I explained, are much easier to change than constitutional provisions, which gives the U.S. system a certain adaptability. "But that's also a vulnerability," I admitted. "What one Congress passes, another can overturn. Constitutional protections are a steeper hill to climb—but once you're there, you're harder to dislodge." But Iraq was starting from scratch with limited institutional memory, minimal infrastructure, and decades of authoritarian rule to overcome.

To avoid being perceived as deflecting from Iraq's challenges, I thought better of mentioning that no system is perfect. That corruption exists at every level in America, too—federal judges, federal prosecutors, FBI agents, DEA agents. It's certainly not rampant; it's rare. Any organization can have bad apples, and when they do, it reflects badly on the whole organization. That doesn't mean the system itself is corrupt. It's the people.

In smaller breakout sessions, maybe twenty officers at a time, the questions came. That's when I started to understand the complexity of what we were attempting. I was teaching about women's rights, discussing domestic violence, and explaining how the law should protect victims. I was told it was the first time the subject had been presented to a mixed audience at the college. The Iraqi Penal Code criminalized rape, sexual assault, and simple assault—all the provisions you'd expect. But then there was Paragraph 41: "There is no crime if the act is committed while exercising a legal right. The following are considered to be in exercise of a legal right: punishment of a wife by her husband."

Punishment. By her husband. Within "limits prescribed by law or by custom."

And Paragraph 128: "The commission of an offense with honorable motives is considered a mitigating excuse." Honor killings, in other words. A man who murdered his sister for shaming the family could argue "honorable motives" and receive a reduced sentence.

This was the law I was teaching police officers to enforce: a constitution that guaranteed women's rights and a penal code that made beating your wife legal.

I made the mistake of referencing the Quran, mentioning that it seemed to tolerate the physical discipline of wives.

One of the male officers stopped me immediately. "No, Leslie," he said, his voice firm but not hostile. "You don't understand. You cannot hit your wife with anything more than a feather. That's what the Quran actually says—only a feather. Physical abuse exists, yes, but not because the Quran endorses it."

I paused, recalibrating. He was educating me, correcting my Western assumptions, teaching me about his own religion in a room where I was supposed to be the teacher. The other officers listened intently, some nodding in agreement. These men seemed genuinely passionate about preventing domestic abuse, about protecting women under the law, about using their authority to enforce justice rather than perpetuate harm.

It was a moment of realization: I'd come here assuming I understood the culture well enough to teach it democratic principles, but I didn't even understand the religious texts that shaped their legal thinking. I was lecturing about imposing Western values while being fundamentally ignorant of the values that already existed.

And yet—we've come a long way in America, even if we're not there yet. I think about my mother's generation—she came from an Irish Catholic family with nine kids. All of the women got married, had children, and stayed home. Not one of them worked outside the house. The number of women now in the workforce, educated professionals—it's increased dramatically in my lifetime. Job opportunities, educational opportunities. I don't know if it's totally equal yet, but the progress has been real.

Iraq was somewhere earlier in that same arc. Laws change faster than cultures do—they always have. Generations have to catch up to what the legal framework already requires of them. I understood that gap personally.

In Japan, I'd worked at a German beer hall to make extra money—little hats, white boots that went up to our knees, serving beer in two-foot-tall glass boots. We were all foreign women, which was the point. One night, a customer grabbed my breast. I slugged him. He went after my manager, broke his glasses, and left him bleeding. And guess who they blamed? Me.

"He was drunk, Leslie. He didn't mean it."

"What do you mean he didn't mean it?"

But that was the system—smile, tolerate, laugh it off. The drunk customer faced no consequences. I was the problem for refusing to accept it.

Maybe that's what I was really trying to teach these Iraqi police officers: not that America had all the answers, but that change was possible—and that it required people willing to say "this is wrong," even when the system told them to stay quiet.

My goal wasn't just to explain the law—it was to teach them to think critically about it, to extrapolate principles rather than simply memorize rules. I'd faced this same challenge teaching in the Philippines, working with students who'd never done hands-on experiments, who wanted to memorize formulas rather than understand the underlying concepts. Martin Luther King once said that the function of education is to teach one to think critically. Intelligence plus character—that is the goal of true education. I believed that deeply.

Back then, I'd give them deliberately false information—"the sky is really red today"—and wait to see if they'd challenge me. Most wouldn't. They'd been trained to accept whatever the teacher said as fact. I'd push them: "Just because I'm the teacher doesn't make it right. The sky isn't red. Think for yourselves."

I taught them wave theory and particle theory, then asked them to apply those principles to phenomena we hadn't explicitly studied. They struggled with it, mystified by the idea that they could predict outcomes based on understanding principles rather than memorizing specific facts. But that was the point—learning to think, not just to obey.

In Iraq, I faced the same dynamic. The officers wanted clear directives: tell us what to do about trafficking, about female genital mutilation, about constitutional violations. They weren't interested in understanding why these laws existed or in applying constitutional principles to situations not explicitly covered by statute. They wanted orders to follow.

But I didn't want them to act solely under the threat of punishment or because an authority figure commanded them. I wanted them to enforce laws because they understood why those laws mattered, because they believed protecting human rights was the right thing to do—not just because Congress *could* withdraw funding if they didn't comply.

"There's no right answer or wrong answer," I'd tell them, "as long as your logic is there."

But logic required a framework. Without a law on the books, they couldn't arrest anybody—that was fundamental. The challenge was getting laws passed, then getting them enforced, then getting people to care about enforcement. I wasn't trying to make them rebels. Police officers in any country must follow the law; that's the foundation of civil society. But I wanted them to think about why laws existed, to recognize how culture, religion, and historical context shape legal frameworks, and to understand what justice actually meant rather than mechanically enforcing whatever statutes happened to be on the books.

That was the real work—teaching them to extrapolate from principles to practice, to internalize democratic values rather than simply performing democratic behaviors under duress. Whether that kind of teaching could take root in a system built on authoritarian obedience, I didn't know. But it seemed more valuable than simply telling them what to do.

There were women police officers too, though not many—just enough to show they were starting to hire them, to acknowledge that a police force needed women to arrest women, to deal with situations where male officers would be inappropriate. The BPC's first all-female class of fifty officers had graduated just three months before I arrived, most of them college-educated, the first women the institution had ever trained for command-level service. One of them let me wear her beret for a photograph, a small gesture of acceptance that meant more than she probably realized. But the lectures felt like performing a strange kind of theater. I'd stand there in my body armor—we could remove our helmets but not our vests—talking about constitutional principles while armed guards surrounded the building and snipers positioned themselves on the roof. The power dynamic was impossible to ignore. I was explaining democratic ideals while representing a military occupation, teaching about equality under law while benefiting from massive structural inequality.

I wondered what they'd think if they knew how I'd come to stand here—that my own path to law had nothing to do with idealism, at least not at first.

***

I'd gone to law school at thirty-seven for a reason I'd kept secret from almost everyone: I wanted to live in Japan permanently.

I'd ended up in Japan almost by accident, teaching, modeling for photographers and national campaigns, acting in commercials, tutoring, translating, whatever brought in money. The income was excellent when everything aligned. I was buying my clothes straight out of Paris. But more than the money, I'd fallen in love with Japanese culture, with its discipline and precision, and with the way social protocols created order out of chaos.

Toshi and I settled into married life in Osaka. He'd started selling real estate—without a license, naturally—and made considerable money. I was piecing together multiple income streams, and when everything aligned, I was making more than I ever could have as a teacher, even though I could only speak Japanese, not read and write it well enough. Japanese has three writing systems: two syllabaries—hiragana and katakana—and kanji, the characters borrowed from China. You need to know around four thousand kanji to graduate from high school. I knew maybe three hundred and fifty. My last job in Japan was as a copy editor for Sumitomo Electric, reviewing their advertising, brochures, and instruction manuals, and helping to rewrite them into proper English. I didn't need to be fluent in written Japanese for that—just fluent enough to understand what they were trying to say.

We had our first son. This was my life now, and I wanted it to stay that way.

In Japan, at least at that time, there was real family stability because divorce was so uncommon. Americans get righteous about affairs—but what follows? The marriage breaks down, there's a divorce, the kids get split up between households, and money becomes an issue. At least in Japan, families stay intact.

If I wanted to stay in Japan permanently, I needed professional credentials that would translate across cultures. Teaching chemistry or physics—my actual training—wouldn't pay enough. A regular teaching job would mean giving up the income I'd been making. Law seemed like the compromise: respectable credentials, the potential for real income, skills that might work in an international context.

Law had been quietly becoming a possibility for years without my realizing it. Even while I was working as a copy editor at Sumitomo Electric, they would come to me when issues arose with DuPont—there had been a long-standing relationship between the companies. Misunderstandings would surface, the kind that happen when two corporate cultures are trying to do business across an ocean, and they'd ask me to intervene. I'd explain where DuPont was coming from, then explain Sumitomo's perspective back to the Americans. I found I was good at it—translating not just language but assumptions, helping each side see what the other actually meant.

I loved that work. It was fascinating, really, to find the logic on both sides and build a bridge between them. No one in my family would have predicted I'd become a lawyer. My father used to tell us, "Never ask a lawyer the time of day—you're going to get a bill for it." My older sister earned two master's degrees and a PhD in biology. My brother went into social work. None of us had any interest in the law or any connection to it.

Law wasn't a calling; it was a pragmatic decision.

I never told Toshi I was taking the LSAT. I didn't mention I'd applied to law schools. I only informed him after I'd been accepted with a scholarship offer. That was how our marriage worked—I made decisions about my career, my education, my trajectory, and he accepted them. Americans always found this arrangement troubling, even incomprehensible. But it wasn't an American marriage operating by American rules. When we lived in Japan, the dynamic made sense in that cultural context. In Connecticut, living with my father after Toshi's family disowned him and forced us to leave Japan, it looked different to outsiders, but the pattern remained the same.

I'd driven to UConn Law School on a moped because we had no money for a second car. I'd study in the law library, and in the early evening, I'd wave through the windows at Toshi when he'd bring the kids to campus. Those waves became a ritual—my connection to normal life while immersed in constitutional law, criminal procedure, and civil rights litigation.

Thankfully, I'd loved the intellectual challenge, the rigor of legal analysis, and the way principles could be applied systematically to complex problems. I'd loved discovering I was good at it, that my science background gave me an analytical edge, and that the methodical thinking required for chemistry translated beautifully to legal reasoning. I'd published in the Law Review as a first-year student, an unusual achievement that gave me the confidence I belonged there despite being older and coming from an unconventional path.

***

Standing in that police college auditorium in Baghdad, teaching constitutional principles to officers who'd lived under dictatorship and were trying to rebuild a functional legal system from the ruins of authoritarian rule, I understood how much easier it had been to study law in a country where democratic institutions already existed and functioned reasonably well.

These officers were trying to enforce laws that had barely been written, to follow constitutional principles that had barely been implemented, and to work in a system where precedent and procedure were still being established. And I was supposed to teach them how it worked based on my American experience, as though democracy could be transplanted like a seedling and expected to grow in completely different soil.

***

The prison visits made the complications even more stark. The freedom to choose my own projects meant I kept looking for places where the work could matter, and the prisons were never far from my mind.

Iraqi detention facilities existed in a strange liminal space between dictatorship-era practices and democratic-era intentions. The laws had changed—women were supposed to be protected, prisoners were supposed to receive humane treatment, and children were supposed to have rights. But the infrastructure, the training, and the culture of enforcement hadn't caught up with the new legal framework. The law said one thing; reality did something else entirely.

In women's detention facilities, I found children living with their incarcerated mothers well beyond the legal limit. The law said children could stay with their mothers until age two, but

I saw six- and seven-year-olds in those facilities, growing up behind bars because no one had anywhere else to put them.

Once we entered the prison grounds, we could move freely among the women and children. We brought food with us, small toys for the kids. A photographer documented the visits—the kind of imagery that made its way into reports and briefings back home. But the conversations that mattered happened off-camera. I talked with the women through our translators: How's everything going? What's happening with your case? How long have you been here? What were you charged with?

These weren't formal interviews—just conversations, the kind that revealed the human reality behind the statistics I was documenting. Women who'd been forgotten by the legal system, children growing up in detention centers because there was no infrastructure to place them elsewhere, families trapped in a system that had changed its laws but not its capacity to implement them humanely.

Inspired by the appalling conditions—sleeping on blanket-covered cement floors, standing in long lines to use a single filthy toilet, and showering in a group once a week; bad food, no sanitary pads, rampant disease, no educational opportunities, no medical or mental health support—I began to ideate.

***

I wanted to establish a legal clinic within the prison—a project I would develop with Iraqi female lawyers and seek State Department funding. In a world of amorphous goals, I wanted something measurable: a legal clinic would be established or not.

I drafted a questionnaire—fifty pages long by the time I finished—to interview the approximately four hundred female detainees at the Rusafa Women's Prison. Demographics, charges, time held in pretrial detention, whether they had counsel, and the nature of their court appearances. I designed it so the data could be entered into a spreadsheet and analyzed. I expected we'd document exactly what we all knew was happening: women arrested on invalid warrants, not timely presented to judges, not provided with court-appointed attorneys, and coerced into signing confessions.

The documents were impressive. The implementation would be another matter.

My argument was simple: the Iraqi Constitution guaranteed a right to counsel. It was right there in the document we'd helped them draft, one of those progressive provisions that made their Constitution look better than ours on paper. But these women weren't getting counsel because they didn't have money. A constitutional right that nobody could afford wasn't a right at all.

In America, we have safety nets. Poor people can apply for aid—medical, financial, legal. A felon getting out of prison might end up doing landscaping or working at Dunkin' Donuts, but there's a system, imperfect though it is. Iraq didn't have that infrastructure. Women left these facilities with nothing—no support, no services, no way to rebuild. Some left without even a Jensiya—Iraq's national identity card, required to access any government service—because no one had been able to establish their citizenship while they were inside.

The clinic would pair Iraqi lawyers with detainees, creating sustainable legal support that would continue after I left. The concept of pro bono service—lawyers donating their time—didn't exist in Iraq. That alone made the project harder than anything I'd done in the States. Whether the funding would materialize, whether the lawyers would commit, whether the system would support it—all uncertain.

It was a small thing in the scope of what we were trying to accomplish in Iraq, but it crystallized something I'd been slowly understanding: the gap between American intentions and American actions, between the democratic principles we championed and the political convenience that often shaped how those principles were actually put into practice.

We were teaching democracy, yes. But we were quite possibly teaching it selectively, emphasizing the parts that aligned with American interests, soft-pedaling the parts that might complicate our strategic goals, sanitizing the reports that might make our involvement look problematic rather than helpful.

And I was starting to understand that teaching people to read the words on paper, to understand constitutional principles, to embrace democratic ideals—none of that mattered if the systems needed to enforce those ideals didn't exist or didn't function.

This was the fundamental challenge we faced in every aspect of our work: believing that changing laws would change reality, that teaching constitutional principles would transform behavior, and that American expertise could transplant democratic institutions into a society deliberately structured to prevent exactly that transformation.

But I was also accumulating a clearer picture of my own limitations. I'd assumed I understood enough about the culture to teach it. The police officer correcting me about the Quran taught me otherwise. I'd assumed legal reform would translate fairly directly into practical change. The children living with their mothers past legal limits, the eight-year-olds being prosecuted for terrorism and related crimes, the remote villages ignoring laws about female genital mutilation, which was another project I was about to take on—all of it taught me otherwise.

But was the occupation itself the problem? Not all occupations had ended the same way.

Japan had fought a formal four-year war that ended in unconditional surrender. Three million Japanese had died. The country was exhausted, ready to try something different. The Emperor himself told his people to accept defeat. We hadn't earned that in Iraq — we'd toppled a government in weeks, leaving a power vacuum and resentment where legitimacy should have been.

The work wasn't wrong. The teaching wasn't misguided. But the context—the foundation we were trying to build on—was fundamentally different from the successful reconstructions I'd studied. And yet—there were moments when the advisory model worked exactly as intended.

***

Part of my assignment was serving as liaison to the Iraqi High Tribunal, the court that had tried Saddam Hussein and his associates. By the time I arrived, most of the major trials were complete, with only a few defendants remaining. But what struck me was that Iraq had done this itself.

There had been enormous international pressure for an outside tribunal—the United Nations, The Hague, the full apparatus of international justice. You could understand the argument: neutrality, legitimacy, the weight of global condemnation. But America had agreed with Iraq that they should try their own dictator. And they had.

The courthouse was extraordinary—a massive stone building where the U.S. had spent millions constructing modern courtrooms. Bulletproof glass protected a huge press gallery. Witnesses testified from behind curtains to protect their identities—something we'd never allow in American courts, but necessary here, where testimony could mean death for yourself and your family. The proceedings were broadcast across Iraq. Hundreds of people were tried. The verdicts were credible. Saddam was executed by hanging (the actual gallows are on display in the Saddam Hussein Museum). Others received long prison sentences. The international community accepted the outcomes.

Iraq had demonstrated it could administer justice on its own terms, for its own people, against its own former leader. That was what advisory work could accomplish when done right: not Americans imposing solutions, but Iraqis building institutions with American support. We were advisors, not occupiers.

But even this success contained a moral failure I couldn't fix. There's a federal law that says if you work for the U.S. government overseas for three consecutive years, you and your entire family can emigrate to America. It's how we protect the interpreters and support staff who risk everything to help us. Our embassy employed thousands of Iraqis—translators, drivers, administrators—and they all qualified. After three years of service, they received permanent U.S. citizenship for their whole family. The tribunal judges didn't qualify.

Think about that. These were the men who had convicted Saddam Hussein. They were targets for anyone who'd supported the old regime. They had to relocate their families into the Green Zone for safety—children pulled out of schools, wives separated from extended family, everyone living in a fortified compound for years while the trials ground on. I was there ten years after the war ended, and there were still trials ongoing. Ten years of their families in lockdown.

But the judges weren't U.S. government employees; they worked for Iraq. So the law that protected our interpreters and others working at the embassy didn't apply to them. The people who'd taken the greatest risk, who'd done what we'd advised them to do: try your own dictator, build your own institutions, demonstrate that Iraqi justice can function—were left to fend for themselves.

I got peripherally involved, trying to help find a legislative remedy. Congress was supposedly working on it; I don't know if they ever did. I never found out what happened to those judges after we left.

Even if the transformation was incomplete, even if the enforcement lagged behind the law, even if some of what we taught would be ignored, corrupted, or lost in translation, some of it would stick. Some officers would remember that the Quran said only a feather. Some judges would remember that children deserved legal representation. Some lawmakers would remember that detention facilities needed medical care and educational programs. That was enough to keep showing up.

CHAPTER 7

INHERITING THE JESSUP LEGACY

The email arrived in early July. The military had started withdrawal weeks earlier, and DePaul's security situation had become untenable.

The withdrawal wasn't sudden—we'd known it was coming. A bilateral security agreement signed three years earlier required all American combat troops to leave Iraq by the end of 2011. The Obama administration had tried to negotiate an extension, offering to keep ten thousand troops for training and support. But the sticking point was immunity: the U.S. insisted any remaining soldiers be protected, under the concept of diplomatic immunity, from Iraqi courts, and the Iraqi parliament wouldn't agree. The Sadr movement—anti-American, politically powerful, and increasingly violent—was staunchly opposed. Prime Minister Nouri al-Maliki, a Shia politician who depended on Sadrist support to hold his fragile coalition together, couldn't deliver the votes. The negotiations collapsed.

So the troops pulled out on schedule, regardless of conditions on the ground. The Special Inspector General for Iraq

Reconstruction had just issued a report calling it a "summer of uncertainty." Iraq was less safe than it had been a year earlier, he said. June had been the deadliest month for American personnel since 2009—fourteen troops killed, the Sadr movement's militia claiming responsibility for over fifty attacks. Rockets were hitting the International Zone more frequently. Assassinations of senior Iraqi officials had reached record levels.

None of this was classified. We read the same news reports everyone else did, watched the same security situation deteriorate around us. What the reports couldn't capture was the feeling of operating in a narrowing window—knowing that American influence was receding, that the infrastructure supporting our work was contracting, that the mission would continue with fewer resources and less protection.

The civilian agencies would remain. The embassy would stay. But everything was about to get harder.

By then, the most dramatic change had already come in how we traveled. For my first months in Iraq, we'd used Rhinos—those massive black armored buses. Then a heat-seeking missile penetrated one of them in Afghanistan, killing everyone inside. The ambassador's response was immediate: no more Rhinos in Iraq. Everything would be by air from then on.

So we switched to helicopters. The embassy compound had its own internal airport, and whenever we needed to travel, we'd show up in full gear to be weighed—us and all our equipment—then board whatever aircraft was available that day. Sometimes it was a small two-passenger helicopter with open doors, the wind so strong it flattened your face. I had the other passenger take a photo of me during one flight, strapped in with the door open, goggles on, my face distorted by the rushing air. As usual, my family was not amused when I sent it home.

Other times, we boarded helicopters that looked like small planes inside—rows of double seats, maybe twenty people, the kind of aircraft I'd never known existed. You never knew what you'd get until you showed up. But it was exhilarating flying low over Baghdad.

From the air, the Green Zone looked exactly like what it was: a fortress inside a city that wanted nothing to do with it. The Republican Palace dominated the compound—one of many of Saddam's palaces, then the military's headquarters, now ours—its bulk unchanged by the succession of occupiers. Near the parade ground, the Victory Arch rose up, two pairs of massive forearms emerging from the earth, clutching crossed swords forty meters long. Saddam had modeled the fists on his own hands, cast from plaster molds. Helmets of dead Iranian soldiers were embedded in the base. It was still standing. No one had decided what to do with it yet.

Beyond the walls, Baghdad sprawled without obvious order. The Baghdad Clock Tower marked the edge of the old city center. The Al-Rasheed Hotel—where journalists had filed their dispatches during the invasion—rose near the zone's perimeter. And somewhere in that maze of streets was the Monument to the Unknown Soldier, a giant tilted shell shape, built in 1982 to honor the dead from the Iran-Iraq War, though by then Saddam had killed far more of his own people than any foreign enemy had.

You couldn't see any of that from inside a Rhino. From a helicopter, it was all visible at once—the whole complicated, layered, still-bleeding city we'd come to help rebuild.

***

We were still absorbing what the withdrawal meant—the mission visibly contracting around us—when the news about DePaul arrived. DePaul Law School was abandoning its contracts. All three of them. Walking away from millions of dollars and leaving Iraq.

The story came out in pieces. There'd been a flaw in DePaul's contract with their security company—something technical that government contract officers had flagged. In Iraq, where American civilian employees couldn't even step outside the Green Zone without armed protection, security contractors were everything. DePaul had to find a new company to take over. But the fired security detail decided to make one final statement: they threatened to ambush the new contractors.

DePaul's response was swift and absolute. They evacuated everyone. Walked away from their entire operation—their secure compound in Baghdad, their substantial staff, their multimillion-dollar contracts. One of those contracts was for the Jessup International Law Moot Court Competition, which Iraq had participated in for the first time the previous year.

Someone would need to take over as National Administrator—someone who could coordinate with Iraqi law schools, find judges, arrange venues, oversee the actual competition, and handle the logistics of getting winning and first-runner-up teams from Baghdad to Washington, D.C., for the international rounds in March. Someone who understood both American and Iraqi legal systems, who could navigate bureaucracy and cultural complexity, and who could manage an international competition they'd never even heard of.

I volunteered before they could finish explaining what it entailed.

When Mark, another DOJ attorney, asked about my moot court experience, I admitted it was limited to law school, twenty-five years earlier, on securities exchange regulations. The looks I received suggested this might not be adequate preparation for administering an international competition involving eighty countries. Mark explained that the Jessup—officially the Philip C. Jessup International Law Moot Court Competition—was the premier international law moot court competition worldwide. The largest and oldest of its kind, it simulated disputes between countries before the International Court of Justice. Law school teams researched and wrote appellate briefs, then presented oral arguments for fictional international law cases. They competed at regional and national levels first, and the top teams advanced to the international championship rounds, which were to be held in Washington, D.C.

The competition was administered by the International Law Students Association and named after former International Court of Justice Judge Philip C. Jessup. The problem was drafted so carefully that no country had an advantage—hypothetical nations with hypothetical laws, ensuring every team competed on equal footing.

Marti Troy from Access to Justice, the USAID implementing partner, emphasized what was really at stake. Iraq had only participated once before, the previous year. This wasn't just about a moot court competition—it was about showing

Iraqi law students they could participate in global legal education, that they belonged in international forums, and that their country's recent history didn't disqualify them from the wider world of legal scholarship.

I told them I could figure it out. The truth was, I had no idea what I was getting into. But that had never stopped me before.

Before I made a single call, I found myself thinking about my own moot court experience—twenty-five years earlier, a different competition entirely. I'd partnered with another student for a securities exchange competition. The topic held zero interest for me—I never did go into securities law—but the competition itself was exhilarating. We'd researched meticulously, prepared exhaustively, and practiced until we could argue either side in our sleep. We made it through the preliminary rounds, then the regional rounds, and finally, the national competition.

We were both articulate. We knew our material cold. But one of the judges—a woman—was just nasty, asking questions that weren't relevant and going out of her way to be hostile. That's not how you're supposed to run a moot court. I knew exactly what she was doing.

I can be a bitch, so I know how to deal with bitches. You ignore it, you answer the question underneath the question, you stay composed, and you don't give them the satisfaction. My partner couldn't do that. He blew up at her. We got kicked out of the competition.

I'd been furious—not at him exactly; I understood that pressure broke people differently—but at the waste of it. We'd been so close. We'd done everything right up until that final moment when composure mattered most.

And now, twenty-five years later, here I was—administering a competition exponentially more complex, involving countries I'd never visited, dealing with logistics I didn't understand, in a war zone where security protocols changed daily. The irony wasn't lost on me.

The Iraqi students needed those skills even more than I did. If participating in an international moot court competition could give them confidence and show them they belonged in global legal discourse, then it was worth every complicated bureaucratic hurdle we'd have to clear.

***

The first challenge was simply understanding the mechanics. I called the International Law Students Association, explained the situation, and they were remarkably understanding—apparently, having your administrators flee a war zone wasn't entirely unprecedented in their experience.

The ILSA representative explained that the problem for the year had already been distributed. Each law school would need to register, pay the fee, select its team, and submit its memorials—the written briefs—by January. Then I'd need to organize the national rounds to determine which teams would represent Iraq in Washington. When I asked how many schools usually participated, she told me it varied by country. I should reach out to all the law schools in Iraq and see who was interested. All the law schools in Iraq. I didn't even know how many that was.

I started making lists: law schools to contact, judges to recruit, venues to secure, funding to arrange. The Department of Agriculture was the official sponsor, meaning they'd cover major expenses such as venue costs and transportation for judges. But the law schools themselves didn't have money for the registration fees, which became another negotiation with ILSA and DePaul.

Then there was the complication of my existing relationships. As National Administrator, I had to maintain complete neutrality. I couldn't favor any school or be seen as giving advantages to teams I knew personally. It meant distancing myself from people I'd worked with, from students I'd taught.

Ali Shaker, my interpreter, would be essential throughout the process. His English was impeccable, and his understanding of legal terminology was sophisticated. But even he couldn't serve as a judge for the practice rounds—we'd both read the bench memorandum, the master document with all the legal analysis judges would need. Anyone who'd seen it was disqualified from judging.

***

I decided to hold the national rounds in Kurdistan, specifically in Erbil. The Anfal campaign I'd read about in training—tens of thousands killed, entire villages destroyed, chemical weapons used against civilians—had happened here. There were photographs in the Saddam Museum of schoolchildren being herded along roads in their bright clothes, Saddam's signature in red ink authorizing atrocities on documents that still existed. The handwriting was careful and deliberate. That was the thing that always stayed with you—how bureaucratic it had been.

By the time I arrived in Iraq, Kurdistan had become the safest region in the country. The contrast with Baghdad was stark. In Erbil, we traveled in two armored vehicles instead of in convoys or helicopters. We didn't have to wear helmets in the car. While we slept on the military base, we worked in an actual hotel—a modern, well-appointed place where normal people went about their normal business—rather than in military compounds. We could walk through the hotel lobby without full protective gear and could see ordinary life happening around us.

That freedom felt like luxury. In Baghdad, we were always conscious of the security protocols, the constant potential for violence, and the separation between us and Iraqi civilian life. In Kurdistan, we could almost forget we were in a war zone. For Iraqi law students from Baghdad and other troubled regions, Kurdistan would offer the same respite. They could focus on international law rather than worry about whether a mortar would hit their hotel.

There was something meaningful about holding this competition in a region that had survived such brutality. Kurdish students would be among those competing, arguing international law principles about justice and human rights in a place where their own people had been denied both for so long.

The venue question solved, I moved on to the next challenge. About twelve law schools expressed interest in participating. Each needed copies of the problem, guidance on memorial writing, and information about the competition format. I sent what felt like hundreds of emails, working through Ali Shaker when language became an issue, trying to make sure every school had equal information and equal opportunity to prepare.

***

By fall, we'd settled on the format. Each school would hold its own internal competition to select its team. Those teams would then compete in the national rounds in Kurdistan. The winner and first runner-up would both get to go to Washington, D.C., for the international rounds.

Getting the judges was easier than I'd expected. DOJ attorneys Mark Wildesen, Marty, and Bessie all volunteered. Marti Troy from Access to Justice also signed on. The team advisors from the various law schools would serve as judges for schools other than their own. Everyone understood what was at stake—not just for the competition, but for the message it sent about Iraq's legal education system.

The Jessup wasn't the only program connecting Iraqi students with American legal professionals. Earlier that spring, I'd arranged for two federal judges from D.C. to visit the law schools—a chance to expose students to how the American judiciary actually worked, to let them ask questions, and see that judges were real people, not abstractions in a textbook.

On a visit to the Green Zone, the Iraqi High Tribunal judges insisted on showing the Americans around. It was embarrassing. These federal judges were distinguished—they'd devoted their careers to the bench. But the Tribunal judges acted like they were receiving minor officials, as if being a U.S. federal trial court judge—one of hundreds in the American system—made them somehow less impressive than the men who'd tried Saddam Hussein. The posturing, the showing off. *My God*, I thought. *Just be gracious.*

Getting them into the Red Zone hadn't been simple. The schedule required the judges to be on the sidewalk in front of the Embassy's apartment building, where they had been lodged when the protective detail arrived, which consisted of six armored vehicles, rather than the usual four, with a helicopter hovering overhead. The female judge was nowhere to be seen. As the case control officer, it was my responsibility to ensure we stayed on schedule, so I'd had to go retrieve her from her room myself. Instead of the four armored limos we usually traveled in, there were six lined up in front with engines running and four military helicopters hovering overhead. Security didn't care about her schedule; they cared about timing. I got reprimanded for that delay—as case control officer, everything was my responsibility.

Our schedule that day was to visit a law school where the federal judges would be on stage before the student body.

Then, mid-session, security pulled us out. There was chatter on the internet about the judges' presence. The female judge understood immediately and moved. The male judge—so accustomed to being the authority in every room—wouldn't listen. I practically had to drag him off the stage while students surrounded him, wanting to talk. He'd had the same training we all had: when the control officer gives an order, you obey instantly. He just couldn't accept that in this context, he wasn't the one in charge. We got out safely.

The experience had taught me something I'd carry into the Jessup: in Iraq, no one got to be the most important person in the room. Not federal judges. Not lawyers from Wachtell Lipton. Not national administrators. The security environment was always the most important thing in the room, and everyone—including me—answered to it.

***

The moot practice rounds were held at the former Reconciliation Center on Prosperity, one of the U.S. military bases being shut down as American forces prepared to leave. It was strange to use these closing military facilities for Iraqi law students to practice international law arguments. The whole enterprise felt like an odd juxtaposition—American military might receding even as Iraqi legal institutions tried to establish themselves in the vacuum.

During the first practice round, the Baghdad College of Law team argued in English. They did well presenting their positions, but when the judges started asking questions, the language barrier became obvious. Answering off the cuff in English while dealing with rapid-fire challenges to their legal reasoning proved too difficult. The team made a unanimous decision: they'd compete in Arabic during the international rounds in D.C. It was allowed—teams could use their native languages—but it meant they'd need interpreters throughout the competition. Just another complication to manage.

***

By December, the law students' memorials had arrived. They'd been drafted in Arabic, but ILSA required English versions to ensure the judges could read them. Ali Shaker certified that his translations accurately reflected the Arabic content. Then it fell to me to edit them.

One hour per page. That was my average. Legal writing is specific and technical in any language; ensuring the English versions maintained the precision and argumentation of the Arabic originals required painstaking attention. The Baghdad College of Law submitted about fifty-five pages. Thi-Qar College of Law submitted about fifty-five pages. One hundred and ten pages of dense legal analysis to edit while managing every other aspect of the competition.

I worked on the memorials during whatever spare time I could find, which was not much. An embassy bombing had taken place during this period, reminding us constantly that we were organizing an academic competition in the middle of a war zone. The incongruity was almost surreal: discussing international law theories while mortars occasionally landed in the compound, editing legal briefs in the same building where we had "duck and cover" drills.

But that was Iraq. Everything important happened against a background of potential violence. You just kept working.

***

The national rounds in Kurdistan drew about twelve law schools. I watched from the administrative side as teams I'd never met argued complex international law cases before judges who'd flown in from various parts of Iraq. The level of preparation varied wildly—some teams had clearly spent months on their research and argumentation, while others seemed to be winging it.

What struck me most was seeing Iraqi women serving as judges alongside the men. Iraq had been the first Arab country to allow female judges—the first appointed in 1959, before many American states had any. But progress had stalled. Of the country's 1,542 judges, only 72 were women—less than five percent. And most of those were confined to family courts and misdemeanors. Only seven worked in criminal courts. Only two sat on appeals courts.

In 1872, the U.S. Supreme Court denied Myra Bradwell the right to practice law in Illinois. "The paramount destiny and mission of woman," the Court wrote, "are to fulfill the noble and benign offices of wife and mother. This is the law of the Creator." That was America, 150 years ago. Not ancient history.

These Iraqi women serving as judges had carved out careers in a system that still saw them as second-class citizens, who were now evaluating the next generation of Iraqi lawyers. They asked sharp questions, challenged weak reasoning, and demanded precision in legal analysis. Watching them work reminded me why this competition mattered—it wasn't just about the students competing but about the entire ecosystem of Iraqi legal education finding its footing in a post-dictatorship world.

After three rounds of competition, the Baghdad College of Law won. The team was all women. The first runner-up was an all-male team from Thi-Qar Law School.

I maintained careful neutrality throughout, even though I'd known several of the young women on the Baghdad team from my earlier work with their law school. Watching them win felt personal in ways I couldn't quite articulate. These were Iraqi women competing in international law, excelling in a field that required them to think critically about governance, justice, and democratic principles. Whatever happened in D.C., they'd already accomplished something remarkable.

The international rounds were still months away. There would be visa applications to submit, memorials to edit, and logistics to arrange. But for now, I watched these young women celebrate their victory and allowed myself to believe the work was worth it.

CHAPTER 8

THE GATE

I stood at the edge of the pool, coffee in hand, watching imported palm trees sway in the morning heat. It was early July, already 115 degrees with a dust storm brewing—the kind of hazy conditions that made mortar attacks more likely. But the pool was empty except for the three of us: me, Connie, an AUSA, and the other Justice Department woman, who'd become my default companions in this place.

We weren't friends in any meaningful sense. We were colleagues who happened to occupy the same narrow band of the vast embassy compound, women who'd gravitated toward each other more from proximity than genuine connection. In the chaos of war-zone work, we grabbed what moments we could—swimming before the heat became unbearable, sitting on the veranda outside the Rec Center with bottled beer, glasses, and an opener we'd buy at the PX because none of us ever remembered to bring one from our apartments.

The pool area itself was its own contradiction: beautiful patio furniture, built-in barbecues, palm trees that could have belonged at any resort, all surrounded by T-walls and bunkers as permanent reminders that we were in Iraq. The pool house was still under construction, materials and equipment scattered around the perimeter. On most mornings, we had the entire facility to ourselves. I soon came to understand why others avoided it—too exposed, too far from the nearest bunker, too much time needed to get from water to safety.

But that morning, standing there with my Nook and coffee, watching the wind pick up dust across the compound, I felt something I hadn't experienced since my Peace Corps days: a moment of almost-normal leisure.

Then the sirens sounded. "Incoming, incoming. Get away from the windows. Take cover. Wait for the all clear."

The same calm, matter-of-fact voice that had become the soundtrack of our lives in Baghdad. Within seconds, the three of us got away from the pool area. We bolted across rough, rocky terrain toward the nearest bunker—all of us in bathing suits and bare feet, dripping wet, moving with the practiced urgency that came from hearing these warnings every few days.

Inside the bunker, we stood there catching our breath, water pooling at our feet, no one saying much of anything. When the all clear finally sounded, I returned to my apartment to change. Before I'd finished pulling on dry clothes, the siren went off again.

After that morning, we never went back to the outdoor pool. The Olympic-sized indoor pool at the rec center was available—it had a hardened roof after people had been killed there in earlier years—but something had shifted. That morning by the outdoor pool marked the last time we'd try to pretend this was anything close to normal.

But the work continued as it always did.

***

Six weeks later, in August, I was in the front passenger seat of one of the embassy cars, with two male colleagues, driving from the embassy compound to the PRT. We'd made this trip together dozens of times—the three of us working together at FOB Prosperity.

Our route took us near one of the main gates into the Green Zone—heavily fortified checkpoints where every vehicle had to stop for inspection. Iraqi guards, American security, barricades and barriers, and blast walls. The gates were choke points, the most vulnerable spots in the entire perimeter. Everyone knew that.

Every time we left the embassy to travel outside the Green Zone, we passed through what felt like an airlock: double walls, a tunnel between them. Even though we were leaving, they still checked the vehicle for explosives. Dogs came and sniffed everything—the vehicle, us.

Coming back was the same ritual in reverse. The huge doors would open. You'd drive in. Those doors would close behind us. The doors in front stayed closed. Only after they'd checked the entire vehicle again—equipment, dogs, the whole procedure—would the inner doors finally open.

All that meticulous security. All those protocols. And yet—

Something arced across the Iraqi sky.

I could see it clearly—a missile, tracing a path overhead. You wouldn't think you'd have time to watch something like that, but everything slowed down the way it does when your brain is trying to process the impossible. The missile descended... and then the explosion came.

The sirens started immediately. That familiar voice: Incoming, incoming. Get away from the windows. Take cover.

We got out of the car. There were people everywhere, all of us converging on the bunkers—those cement tunnel structures scattered strategically throughout the Green Zone. They were maybe twelve feet long, not very high. Even I, at five feet two inches, couldn't stand up straight inside them. But they were hardened cover, and hardened cover was what you wanted when missiles were falling.

All that physical training I'd done before deployment—the weight loss, the preparation, the West Virginia driving course—none of it mattered in that moment. Adrenaline took over. Getting to a strategically placed bunker didn't require the ability to do weighted squats or run obstacle courses. It just required moving. Your body knows what to do when survival is at stake. The training had been about liability, I realized—the government could say they'd prepared us. But when a missile is falling, you don't think about technique. You just go.

I managed to squeeze into one of the tunnels, but most people couldn't—there were too many of us, and everything was happening too fast. You're just reacting. You don't think. You move.

The explosion at the gate was about thirty feet from where we'd been. Maybe less. Close enough that I could feel it, that my ears rang with it.

We waited for the all-clear. Thirty minutes. Maybe forty. Time moves strangely when you're crouched in a cement tunnel, wondering if another missile is coming.

Back in training in D.C., we'd spent a full day on situational awareness. Four of us in a van, driving around in the snow, looking for anything unusual: a woman walking down the street with only one boot on (it turned out she was a suspicious threat); a box sitting on a snowbank—why would someone leave that there? (It turned out to be an explosive device.) We went to a restaurant for lunch, where some of the other diners were actors playing bad guys. We had to observe everyone without making it seem like we were observing. At the end of the day, they debriefed us on all the threats we'd missed, all the clues we'd failed to notice. The whole idea was that you needed situational awareness in Iraq; you never knew what was going to happen.

Apparently, a missile at the gate.

Nobody was panicking, exactly. We'd all been through the training, had all heard the sirens before.

***

After the pool incident, I'd stopped getting out of bed for the nighttime alerts—the crystal-clear desert air made daylight attacks unlikely, so the mortars usually came at dusk or dawn or during dust storms when visibility dropped. You learned to calculate the odds, to pull the quilt over your head, and go back to sleep.

But the attacks had been increasing. Rockets were hitting the International Zone, the embassy compound—more than before. That week alone, we'd had duck-and-cover alerts almost every day. It was no coincidence: Vice President Biden and Admiral Mullen were in Baghdad, hammering out negotiations about whether any American troops would remain past the December deadline. The Sadr movement knew exactly what was at stake. While diplomats talked, their militia was sending its own message. Militant groups were taking advantage of the withdrawal timeline, and this was the window—with 47,000 American troops leaving by year's end, the pressure was on to make the cost of staying as visible as possible. Everyone knew it: the insurgents, the militias, us.

The numbers told the story plainly enough for anyone paying attention. The Special Inspector General for Iraq Reconstruction had just issued his assessment: Iraq was less safe than it had been a year earlier. June had been the deadliest month for American personnel since 2009. April through July had seen the highest number of assassinations of senior Iraqi officials since anyone had started tracking the figures. The Inspector General called it a summer of uncertainty. From inside the compound, it felt less like uncertainty than like a clock running down.

Weeks earlier, someone had managed to plant a bomb under the floor of a trailer used as an office in the Rusafa complex—the site of the police college and prisons where DOJ personnel worked regularly and where I'd been going myself. The Justice Department had far more police officers in Iraq than attorneys, and I'd gotten to know several of them. That morning, the interpreter entered the trailer first and detonated the device. He was killed. Others were injured. The Ambassador shut it down immediately—not just that office, but the entire Rusafa complex. All those sites I'd been visiting regularly were off-limits now.

The wall in the main embassy building made the cost visible in another way. There was a huge foyer with one massive wall near the ambassador's office. We'd seen the wall for the first time during training: it carried the names of every American civilian who'd been killed, a growing memorial to the price we were paying. But the atmosphere changed. The rules got stricter. We needed even more protection. The sense of vulnerability was no longer theoretical.

The message was clear: collaboration with Americans could get you killed, whether you were American or Iraqi. And yet people kept showing up.

Then came the gate. This wasn't a mortar landing somewhere across the compound. This was a missile. This was people dying just yards from the PRT where we worked.

***

When the all-clear finally sounded and we made it to the PRT, photographs and videos were already on the TV monitors. Someone had tuned the TVs to the local feed, and there it was: the gate, the aftermath, the cleanup.

Bulldozers.

They were already there, maybe thirty minutes after the explosion, recovering the injured and the dead, shoveling debris. Crumpled cars. Wreckage. Just shoveling everything out of the way so traffic could get through the gates.

I stood watching the screen, and something in me went very still.

I'd spent six years as a federal prosecutor in New Haven, building cases where the evidence was everything. Hornbook law: photograph the scene, document the positions, collect the fragments that tell you what kind of explosive was used, where it was placed, and what vehicle carried it. Interview witnesses while their memories are fresh. That's how you catch the people responsible. And that was precisely what we were here to teach.

And there on the screen, bulldozers were pushing the evidence into piles of rubble.

No investigators taking photographs. No one collecting fragments or documenting blast patterns. No one asking what kind of explosive, what vehicle, what entry point. People had been killed—their bodies were out there—and the response was to clear the debris so cars could get through.

One of my colleagues said what we were all thinking: "What the hell are we even doing here?"

The UN had just issued its human rights report: an over-reliance on confessions to convict, it said, encourages an environment where the torture of detainees takes place. Why collect evidence when you can beat a confession out of someone? And ending impunity, the report noted, remained a serious challenge—perpetrators of crimes committed over many years continuing to be unaccountable.

But this wasn't a crime with an unknown perpetrator. Everyone knew which side had done it—the adversaries were known to each other, attacks met with retaliation, in an open-ended cycle that had nothing to do with evidence or prosecution. You don't build a case against the other side of a war. So the bulldozers weren't just a failure of forensics training. They were a reminder of what we were actually operating inside: not a rule-of-law reconstruction project, but a war that hadn't finished deciding what it was.

Here, at a gate where people died, there was no evidence because no one collected it. There would be no investigation because no one conducted it. There would be no consequences because there was nothing to build a case on. We were watching impunity in real time.

Maybe it was fatalism. *Inshallah.*

***

We finished the drive to the PRT. We did our work. We ate dinner at the DFAC and made small talk about things that didn't include bulldozers clearing bodies from checkpoints. The routines absorbed the horror, as they always did.

We'd come to Iraq to teach them how to build a justice system. Preserve the evidence. Build the case. Hold people accountable. And when people died at the gate, we watched bulldozers clear the scene so traffic could move.

That was the work. That was what we were doing here.

CHAPTER 9

SURFACE AND DEPTH

Around six months into my deployment, the PRT program officially ended. The military had basically withdrawn back in June; now the Provincial Reconstruction Teams were closing too. We would all work exclusively from the embassy compound from now on. No more driving to FOB Prosperity in the morning, grabbing keys from the box, joking with other agencies about overlapping projects.

What I lost most wasn't security—it was visibility into what everyone else was doing. At FOB Prosperity, I knew what Agriculture was working on, what Finance was tackling. If there were an extra seat in a convoy, I could tag along on projects like the wheelchair distribution and see the work from different angles. At the embassy, we worked in separate office buildings. The fun things disappeared—those spontaneous collaborations, the cross-agency exchanges that made the mission feel coherent rather than isolated.

The truth was, we'd barely seen the military even when they were here. When the outlying bases closed, they didn't abandon the embassy—there was still a huge military presence on the compound. They had separate quarters elsewhere—barracks or tents, nothing like our apartments—and we inhabited different worlds despite sharing the same two-mile stretch along the Tigris.

But our paths crossed mainly at the DFAC or on Thursday and Friday nights when we'd all converge at Baghdaddy's—the Rec Center that was used as a bar that also served as a movie theater, meeting venue, and chapel depending on the day.

At Baghdaddy's, groups volunteered to tend bar every couple of months. Music came from whoever could play. When it was the Rule of Law group's turn, we fielded six DOJ attorneys, an ATF staffer, and a U.S. Marshal. My assignment: making popcorn.

There were no guns allowed. Zero tolerance for anything that looked like aggression—one military guy stumbled on the stairs leaving one night and was sent home before morning. Everyone had to stay calm, stay smooth, stay happy. In a compound full of attorneys trained to manage conflict, we weren't allowed to have any.

That disappeared too.

At FOB Prosperity, we'd adopted a stray cat—the only pet any of us had. When the PRTs closed, one of the local Iraqis took her. Back on the embassy compound, pets were not allowed. No animals of any kind, really. No ants. No mosquitoes. No flies. Even the natural world had been sterilized out.

The only dogs were the 103 explosives-detection dogs that checked our vehicles at the gates—and we only saw them from inside the car, windows up, as they circled and sniffed. So when "Meet the Dogs Day" was announced, I signed up immediately. We watched demonstrations. We learned about their training and how they worked 48-hour weeks in 2-hour shifts, each with its own handler.

And we were allowed to pet them. That was the kind of thing that passed for joy in the compound. Petting a dog.

The small conveniences we'd learned to enjoy disappeared one by one. The Subway counter closed its window. Then the pizza place. The Green Bean coffee shop went dark. These weren't security threats—they were just services that depended on the military presence and the customer base it provided. Without them, the amenities contracted back to what the embassy staff alone could sustain.

The supply chain problems went beyond closed businesses. Convoys couldn't get through as reliably without military escorts. The moment military protection disappeared, Iraqi officials started finding pretexts to delay trucks at checkpoints—a supposed mistake on a license plate, some made-up regulation. Here we were, doing our best at the embassy, trying to help their country, and this was the thanks we got. It sounds petty to admit now, but it stung.

One week, it was Diet Coke. Can you believe that? No Diet Coke. People who relied on their three cans a day started hoarding them from the DFAC, stuffing their pockets to stockpile in their apartments. Then, toilet paper became scarce. People began stealing rolls from public restrooms. The absurdity of it—professional attorneys and diplomats reduced to petty theft over basic supplies.

The routines continued—wake, work, DFAC, sleep—but something was shifting. I'd learned that the dining facility was staffed by 230 men, mostly from India, Nepal, and Sri Lanka, paid $450 a month. The manager ordered $240,000 worth of food every five days to feed 1,400 breakfasts, 2,300 lunches, and 2,000 dinners. One hundred of those men were leaving Iraq shortly after three years in the country without a single break because leave resulted in a loss of pay. Three years of peeling our mangoes, cooking our lobster, washing our dishes. Three years inside the same walls, while others complained after twelve months.

The compound had always been isolated, but that isolation was deepening in ways we couldn't yet fully see.

***

The three Justice Department women I'd spent time with saw each other less as these changes took hold. We'd never been close, not really. The woman with young children back home took all three R&Rs so she could get back every few months. The other attorney worked in a completely different legal area—I barely understood what her cases involved. Connie Bowden was an AUSA from Pittsburgh on her second detail in Iraq, which made her, by default, my closest friend there. "There wasn't a lot of competition for the position," I might have said.

Even so, we knew job titles, general family situations, and home states. We could recognize each other's routines, predict who'd show up at the DFAC at what times. But we rarely talked about anything substantive. There wasn't time, and maybe there wasn't energy.

My living situation reflected the same pattern—proximity without intimacy. I ended up with a roommate, a nice woman from Diplomatic Security, a polygraph examiner who spent her days conducting security clearance interviews and polygraph examinations. It should have been a natural connection—I'd worked extensively with polygraphs when I headed the asset forfeiture unit in Connecticut.

My FBI colleague and I had pioneered the use of polygraph exams to identify "innocent owners" in drug cases. We offered the test to people, like the Derbackers, who claimed they didn't know their house was being used for drug dealing. If they proved truthful on the two relevant issues—that is, they had not used the property for drug trafficking and were unaware of others using it—we released their property.

The technique made my FBI colleague and me minor celebrities in federal law enforcement circles. We traveled the country lecturing on it—prosecutors, agents, banking groups, and bar associations—explaining how a simple polygraph could separate the truly innocent from those hiding behind plausible deniability.

But my roommate and I never talked about any of that. We never ate dinner together. We never had a drink on the veranda.

It's strange, looking back—I'm an open, friendly person who loves talking to almost anyone. Yet we were like two strangers who happened to sleep in the same apartment. We had our missions, our exhausting days, and our separate routines. The apartment was just where we collapsed between shifts.

For some, this may sound lonely, but for me, it felt normal.

***

In Japan, there's a relationship concept called *sotsukon*—sometimes translated as "marriage graduation." It means a couple stays legally married but stops living like a traditional pair, allowing each person to enjoy more independence. The idea, often associated with writer Yumiko Sugiyama's 2004 book, describes a way to keep the stability of marriage while reshaping the relationship to fit new goals, especially later in life.

Toshi and I had been living some version of this arrangement for years before I'd ever heard the term. When our kids were still young, we settled into a pattern—he'd come down to D.C. on weekends, and we'd do things together, but during the week, I was essentially on my own.

Somewhere in there, I ended my marriage to Toshi. If I were going to D.C., I might as well cut him loose so he could live his life and I could live mine. Our kids were older and out of the house.

The work consumed everything. I'd wake up with my color-coded memo book—stars for priorities, blue and red categories, tasks checked off as completed—and move through the day with military precision. Morning meetings. Before the military left, convoys to Baghdad law schools, prison visits, and lectures on democratic principles to police officers. Legal reform initiatives that required navigating bureaucracies I barely understood. Back to the embassy by dark, dinner at the DFAC, maybe an hour before collapsing into bed.

The women around me operated the same way. We'd see each other at meals and coordinate schedules for overlapping projects. But we didn't linger. We didn't share confidences. We certainly didn't become the kind of friends who'd travel together after this was over, who'd exchange letters for decades, or who'd serve as each other's family at life milestones.

We were survival companions, not soul mates. And maybe that was all any of us had the capacity for in a place like this.

It was nothing like my Peace Corps friendships.

***

In the Philippines, Linda and I taught at the same university. She was Filipino, a local teacher, the youngest of maybe ten or twelve kids in her family. We became best friends, though I couldn't tell you exactly why. We just clicked. She had a real adventurous streak—it took us months to get her a passport, bribes to corrupt officials, and endless bureaucratic run-arounds. But she was determined.

When my Peace Corps service ended, Linda and I traveled to Japan on the strength of that casual invitation from a Japanese student—his father had a guest house, he'd said, and would love to host us.

Linda's language skills saved us during those first awkward days at Mr. Oku's house. She spoke the three national languages—English, Spanish, and Tagalog—plus several regional dialects; she could communicate enough to smooth over the shock of our arrival.

Mr. Oku let us stay about three weeks before gently suggesting we might be more comfortable at Shinoji Temple in central Osaka, where there was a dormitory for foreign students.

Shinoji was perfect—the largest temple in Osaka, hundreds of acres. The hereditary priest had married an American woman. He had also built the dormitory. Linda and I each got our own small apartment—a bedroom, tiny kitchen, and shared bath. Right in the center of a city of six million people, with subway access and opportunities everywhere.

We taught English at the YMCA, gave private English lessons, and worked illegally on tourist visas until we could get proper work permits. I also moonlighted at that German beer hall, where the owners hired white women specifically for the Bavarian fantasy—short skirts, velvet bustiers, and beer in two-foot-tall glass boots. Linda, despite being just as desperate for work, was excluded because of her dark skin.

We went through Japan together, but not identically. We both, however, ended up marrying Japanese men, which was especially remarkable for Linda, whose older sisters remembered hiding in the attic when Japanese soldiers invaded the Philippines, terrified of being raped.

By the way, we didn't learn the true story of Mr. Oku until Linda's wedding, about two years after we'd arrived in Japan. Even for love marriages in Japan, you need a "go-between"—two people who sit at the head table and give speeches about the couple. Linda chose Mr. and Mrs. Oku.

That's when we heard it. The go-between's speech was supposed to tell the couple's story, and Mr. Oku told the truth: how his son had never mentioned us, about the telegram from me arriving without warning, and how he'd gone to the authorities, genuinely believing we were criminals trying to infiltrate Japan. The investigation turned up nothing. And despite his fear, despite every rational reason to refuse, he'd picked up these two strange women at the airport and taken them to his home.

My father was Linda's best man. He stood up for her at that wedding and couldn't believe what his daughter and Linda had done—showing up unannounced at a stranger's house halfway around the world, taking a casual comment from a college student as a binding invitation.

Linda stayed in Japan and had two kids. One became an international badminton player. We remained friends until her death—she was someone with whom I had traveled, taken risks, and built a life alongside. Someone whose history I knew, whose choices I witnessed, whose wedding I attended, and whose children I watched grow up.

That was what real friendship looked like. Someone who'd be there when you did something crazy and impossibly naive. Someone who'd learn a language with you, work illegally with you, and figure out life in a foreign country with you. Someone whose family's trauma you understood, whose courage you admired, and whose loyalty you could count on for decades.

We knew virtually none of that about each other in Iraq. Maybe that was protective in an environment where the mission kept shifting, people kept coming in, then leaving when their time was up. Or maybe we just didn't have the energy for a deeper connection because we were all working so hard. We had a single year to make our mark.

***

The military withdrawal made even our limited companionship more difficult to sustain. I buried myself in the international moot court competition, just as I had during police training sessions and in prison visits that revealed the inadequacies of the juvenile justice systems I sought to reform.

Maybe I wasn't built for casual friendship because I'd witnessed the alternative. I'd seen what real loyalty looked like under complicated circumstances.

Within a year or two after my mother's death, my father married Louise—Louise Number Two, we called her, since my mother's name had also been Louise. She was a nurse, an Irish Catholic woman with a daughter, Joanne, from a previous marriage.

Joanne and I were the same age, shared a bedroom, and became inseparable. She had blonde hair and blue eyes like my dad, so everyone thought I was the adopted one.

But Louise Number Two was bipolar and an alcoholic. Her mood swings were violent and unpredictable. My father, who never once physically punished any of us, who insisted our language stay civil, and who believed in reasoning through problems—this gentle, thoughtful man found himself managing complete chaos.

At one point, it got so bad that my father rented an apartment. He told us kids, "Just take a suitcase; we're not taking anything else." It was natural that Marilyn, a year and a half older than me, David, three years younger, and I would leave. And yet, when Joanne heard this, she told her mother, "I'm going with my father." Louise tried to stop her. "You're my daughter," she said. Joanne was clear: "No, I'm going with my father."

We loved our apartment in Hartford, not far from St. Joseph's Cathedral School, which we attended through our freshman year in high school. For the first time, Joanne and I could see our friends after school. We bought all the bedding, curtains, dishes, pots, and pans—we had a ball. We stocked up on Coke and potato chips. No more loud voices, no more yelling. Just peace.

We told my dad, "We don't need a nice house; this little apartment is just fine."

But my father went back to West Hartford almost every evening to check on Louise, to make sure she was still alive. After three or four months, he decided we should move back. We said to him, "Get a divorce."

I remember his response, word for word: "If she had cancer, would you want me to leave her?"

We said no, of course not.

"Well," he said, "mental disease is just the same."

That's where I learned about loyalty, about commitment that goes beyond what's easy or comfortable, about staying when things get hard.

After Louise died of cancer, my father lived alone in the West Hartford house.

My father's loyalty extended even to providing for Joanne long after Louise had died. Years later, when Joanne was married, had two kids, and struggled financially, he changed his will to make Joanne the sole beneficiary, giving her the house—a paid-off, four-bedroom place in West Hartford. He wrote to me, Marilyn, and David to let us know. None of us cared; we were all doing fine professionally. But Joanne was needy—she'd married right out of high school. At the time, Bob, her husband, delivered oil for his stepfather's oil company. My father invited Joanne and her family to live with him.

The remarkable thing? My father never told Joanne about the will. He didn't want her to feel indebted to him or to stop trying to find their own home. That was the kind of person he was—looking after people who needed help while preserving their dignity.

Joanne remained my closest friend. At one point, while living with my dad, still uncertain about our ability to return to Japan and neither of us working, I left my two young children to study in Southeast Asia for ten weeks. Joanne was the one I trusted completely. She was the steady one, the responsible one, the soft place for my kids to land. We stayed friends until she died too young, due to complications from diabetes gone undiagnosed for years—not just because she was my sister; she was also my confidant.

I carried those lessons into my marriage with Toshi. For instance, when I mentioned to him that I wanted to take that ten-week college course on Southeast Asia Studies, even though it was costly and would require me to be far away, he readily agreed. In part, because he wanted to fit into American society and assumed that was a cultural norm. What I liked best was that I got my way with the house, the kids, and the vacations.

I'm a control freak, which worked perfectly within the Japanese household structure—everything within the house is controlled by the woman. Every vacation, I planned. Discipline, school, everything. Once we were out at a restaurant, and Cary was maybe five years old, he put his elbow on the table. Toshi said, "Lee, tell him to take his elbow off the table." So I said, "Cary, take your elbow off the table." Toshi was sitting right next to him, but he couldn't say it himself. That's the mom's job.

In Iraq, there was no such structure—no defined roles, no household logic to default to. Just a compound full of people getting through the day.

Those colleagues at the pool, on the veranda, in that dynamic we'd created? We weren't built for that kind of depth.

***

The contrast became clearer when I left the compound.

I used every day of my R&R allotment—66 days total over three trips—and each one reminded me what real connection looked like.

I'd actually tried to take fewer trips. I applied for a waiver to combine my allotment into two longer R&Rs instead of three shorter ones—it would save the government money. The request was summarily denied. The rationale, as I understood it, was for mental health reasons: three opportunities to get out of a war zone. So I booked the October safari and used every day I was entitled to.

Some people at the embassy didn't take trips. They said they couldn't afford it, or they didn't want to deal with the logistics. The two-day journey out, the two-day journey back in—it left only 18 days in the actual destination. I couldn't understand that mindset. Here at the embassy, we had little to distract us from work—no family, no friends, no restaurants, no coffee shops, no pets. R&R wasn't a vacation; it was the only reminder that a different life existed.

For one of my R&Rs, I went on safari in Kenya. I invited my son, Miki, his wife, Tiffany, and my granddaughters, Melanie and Audrey. My cousin Cindy flew in from North Carolina. I rented a private house overlooking a watering hole in the Mara North Conservancy—all stone and cedar, with a swimming pool, two cooks, two maids, and our own guide named Salaash. We'd gather on the veranda in the evening to plan the next day's adventures while watching animals come to the watering hole.

We took a hot air balloon ride over the Kalahari Desert. Audrey was too young to join us, so Salaash let her "drive" the vehicle through the desert. He let her sit in his lap and steer the 4x4 as he followed the basket to its landing site. She was four years old, completely serious about the job.

One afternoon, Salaash took us unannounced to a Masai village—no appointment, no warning. The village elder came out to meet us anyway, along with his wives and children. Melanie and Audrey were an immediate sensation, surrounded by kids their own age who'd never seen children who looked like them. The welcome was instant and total, the kind that has nothing to do with shared language. We saw giraffes, lions, and rhinos. After a week, Miki and his family returned to Germany.

Cindy and I went on to Egypt—Cairo, Alexandria, Aswan, Luxor, Abu Simbel. We took the overnight train, cruised the Nile, and rode a hot air balloon over ancient ruins.

***

When I returned to Iraq after each R&R, the contrast hit harder. Out there, I'd been with people who knew me—really knew me. Family. Old friends. People I'd choose to spend time with anywhere. Back on the compound, I slipped back into those careful, cordial exchanges with colleagues, the same surface conversations.

The pool where we'd gone that July morning stayed empty. We told ourselves we'd go back when things settled down, but they never did. The veranda where we'd drunk beer and watched the sunset went unused. The small rituals that had created the illusion of normalcy were fading. We drifted into separate orbits. Years later, I'd struggle to remember most of their names. Connie, yes. One or two others. But not their stories, not their motivations for volunteering for Iraq. Everyone else? Colleagues. Friendly. Cordial.

I returned my focus to the work itself: the legal reforms, the training, the moot court competition—the things I'd actually come to accomplish.

CHAPTER 10

CHILDREN IN THE SYSTEM

After the PRT program ended, I was reassigned to work as the Grants Officer Representative for a UNICEF project called "Strengthening Protection and Justice for Children and Young People in Iraq." The title was bureaucratic and clinical. The reality was something else entirely.

The project addressed what UNICEF called violations of the United Nations Convention on the Rights of the Child—a document Iraq had actually signed. The treatment of children in Iraq's criminal justice system didn't just fail to meet international standards; it didn't even comply with Iraq's own laws. Children as young as nine years old could be held criminally responsible under Iraqi law. In Kurdistan, the age was eleven. They faced arrest and long periods of pre-trial detention regardless of the nature of their alleged offense. They had no due process protections worth mentioning, no rehabilitation programs, and no alternatives to custody.

I'd already seen some of this during my visits to the Rusafa Women's Prison earlier in the year. I'd seen vulnerable Iraqi children before, including the eight-year-old boy who'd never been in a sitting position in his life until we gave him a wheelchair at the distribution event. But now it was my job to coordinate the State Department's response through UNICEF's implementing partners, to monitor programs designed to change these conditions, to review progress reports, and to ensure compliance with grant terms.

Officially, my role included "site visits and liaison with the recipient." In practice, I was unable to visit any of the juvenile detention facilities due to security restrictions. My plan to train the attorneys retained to represent the detainees was never executed—logistics and security made it impossible. I was responsible for monitoring a project I couldn't observe, evaluating programs I couldn't see.

The project had four objectives: prevent children from coming into contact with the law through community programs; protect children in pre-trial detention; restore justice; and reintegrate released children with their families and communities. The goal was to enhance the capacity of over 400 "duty bearers"—juvenile judges, prosecutors, detention facility staff, including social workers, guards, and care providers—to provide better legal, judicial, rehabilitation, and reintegration services to the approximately 1,200 boys and 100 girls in detention facilities.

That was the language of the grant documents. The reality was messier, more frustrating, and far more heartbreaking.

I documented these conditions meticulously, writing detailed reports on overcrowding, inadequate sanitation, lack of medical care, and the absence of educational or vocational programs.

Each year, the State Department submits Country Reports on Human Rights Practices to Congress—factual, country-by-country assessments prepared by U.S. diplomats that carry real consequences: foreign policy decisions, foreign aid, sanctions, and asylum determinations all draw on them. I contributed the section on juvenile detention for the year I was there, laying out the facts without editorializing and providing concrete numbers and specific observations.

Before I drafted my section, I went back and read the 2011 Human Rights Report on juvenile detention in Iraq. It was 119 words long. It described facilities as "improved," populations "within capacity," and stated there were "no reported instances of abuse or mistreatment in any of the facilities." Legal, medical, educational, and social services were listed as available on-site.

I knew that information was false. The data I was seeing told a completely different story. I submitted 1,464 words of facts. No editorializing. Just data.

What ultimately appeared in the published report was fifty-seven words long. The careful documentation I'd provided had been reduced to a sanitized summary that bore little resemblance to what I'd actually observed.

I sent an email to the State Department officer responsible: "I will not comment on the detention paragraph. I do not want my name associated with it in any way. In my opinion, it is inaccurate and misleading."

Then I sent a follow-up because the anger wouldn't settle: "I provided you with the most accurate information that I had available to me. I obviously have no objection to summarizing what I wrote. In my opinion, that is not what was done... If you think I feel strongly about this, I do. I spent considerable effort writing that section, and having handled asylum litigation on behalf of the U.S. Justice Department for one year, I am very aware of the extent to which administrative judges and DOJ attorneys rely on the accuracy of the State Department Reports in taking positions on asylum eligibility."

The response was polite, bureaucratic, and unmoved. The report would stand as written.

***

It wasn't the first time I'd encountered authorities who preferred a sanitized version of events to an accurate one. I'd learned that years earlier in Birčko, Bosnia — the only town not awarded to either side under the Dayton Peace Accords, still crawling with UN personnel, still laced with landmines on many unpaved surfaces. Nothing was open. The library sat half-destroyed. We walked only on pavement and counted ourselves lucky.

One day, four of us volunteers — including a member of the Canadian Parliament — walked toward the U.S. military base along a road lined with skeletal buildings. Red brick houses, mostly, every window gone, every door removed, people having scavenged the wood, the glass, everything of value. Bare bones, like a zebra after lions have finished with it.

I was taking photographs when two local policemen stopped us. "You are forbidden from taking photographs."

I whipped out my official ID. "I'm an American prosecutor, and I'm going to take these photos."

Everyone except the Canadian fled. The police let us pass after I asked to see their IDs.

I'd researched the locations of three mosques that had stood in the city before the war. One was now a park; another, a parking lot; the third, just rubble. They hadn't simply closed these mosques—they'd obliterated them, removed every brick, erased all evidence. I wasn't photographing piles of rubble like you see on television; I was documenting something more insidious: the methodical erasure of a people, structure by standing structure.

I was foolhardy that day, but I was outraged by the attitude that the world should not see what had happened here—that horror should be kept quiet rather than witnessed and recorded. I had a responsibility to share what I saw. I didn't care about safety in that moment. The FBI agent who'd called me a "junkyard dog" would have recognized the look on my face.

***

That same instinct—to document everything, insist on accuracy, and refuse to let inconvenient truths disappear—was exactly what the UNICEF assignment required of me.

I'd prepared for this assignment by reviewing every relevant document I could find: the UN Convention on the Rights of the Child, the Beijing Rules for juvenile justice, Iraq's own Juvenile Care Law, reports on institutional violence against women and girls, and the Iraqi Penal Code provisions pertaining to juveniles.

I met with UNICEF's Chief of Child Protective Services and the country director of the implementing partner organization. I was as prepared as I could be for an assignment I could not actually see. The project existed on paper, funded by American taxpayers and monitored through reports and meetings, while the children it was meant to help remained largely invisible to me.

In Iraq, my instinct to prepare, to act, and to measure progress—that drive constantly ran up against limitations. Security restrictions meant downtime—lots of it. The UNICEF project was the ultimate expression of that frustration: I had responsibility for monitoring programs I couldn't visit, for ensuring accountability when I couldn't see the actual work, and for representing American commitment to children I was prohibited from meeting. This drove me absolutely mad.

So I focused on what I could control: the documentation, the reports, the insistence on accuracy. I wrote detailed accounts of what the implementing partners reported, what UNICEF observed, and what the numbers revealed about a system that was failing its most vulnerable population.

The numbers told their own story. Detention centers designed for thirty held fifty-five. Boys slept on floors next to toilets with no pillows because guards feared they'd suffocate each other. Girls were not allowed to use the toilets after dinner. They wet their beds. Five toilets for 150 children. No educational programs. No vocational training. Medical care that existed in theory but rarely in practice.

And the charges themselves revealed something darker than simple institutional failure: children arrested for carrying explosive devices they didn't understand they were carrying; children prosecuted for sex crimes when they were clearly victims rather than perpetrators; children whose parents had sent them on errands that turned out to be criminal activities, collecting payment while the children faced prosecution.

While some parents were arrested, the adults had a right to an attorney under Iraqi law. The children did not. This created an immediate conflict of interest in every case. If a ten-year-old was carrying munitions because an adult told him to transport a package, who was the criminal? Iraqi law treated the child as the perpetrator. The parent who'd handed him the package, who knew exactly what was inside and who had likely been paid for the delivery—that adult, if faced with charges, had the right to be represented by counsel. The child faced years in detention. They had no legal representation, no understanding of their rights, and no advocate of any kind. The concept of children's rights was completely foreign in a legal system that had functioned under dictatorship for decades.

The obstacle wasn't simply that children lacked attorneys; it was that Iraqi law required parental consent before a child could be represented by counsel. Over half of the children in detention were charged with terrorism-related crimes. The parents who had sent them on those errands and who had handed them the packages were hardly inclined to consent to legal representation that might expose their own involvement. There was no provision in Iraqi law for a judge to appoint an attorney to represent a child's interests without that consent. The parents held the key, but most chose not to use it.

The numbers told their own story in another way, too. Of the most recent ninety-five juvenile detainees who went to trial, seventy-six percent were acquitted. These children had been held for months—sometimes years—on insufficient evidence. The system hadn't detained them because they were guilty. It had detained them because it could.

***

My own son, Miki had been a sophomore at Glastonbury High School, playing eight musical instruments, performing in a private string quartet, and fielding invitations to apply to prestigious universities. He was brilliant—and like many brilliant teenagers, capable of spectacularly poor judgment. He built a bomb in our basement. Not because anyone told him to, not because he was a courier for adults with violent intentions. He built it because he was curious, smart, and sixteen.

Then he brought it to school, put it in his own locker, and detonated it.

The consequences were serious: expulsion, transfer to a school for troubled kids, and the end of his trajectory toward elite universities. He only graduated because he'd accumulated so many extra credits. But he wasn't arrested. He wasn't thrown into an adult prison. He wasn't held for years without legal representation. The system recognized—as American juvenile justice generally does—that teenagers do profoundly stupid things and that a single act of adolescent recklessness shouldn't define a life.

These Iraqi children hadn't even done anything stupid. They'd done what adults told them to do. They'd carried packages without knowing what was inside. And for that, they faced years in facilities with no rehabilitation, no education, and no path back to normal life.

Miki's bomb incident wasn't the only time I watched the American system protect a minor from consequences that, in Iraq, would have been crushing.

I was upstairs in the federal courthouse in New Haven when my secretary told me the Associated Press was on hold. I assumed they wanted a comment on something happening in the courtroom. Instead, the reporter said, "We're calling to get your reaction to your son's drug arrest."

My son's drug arrest. He was a minor. I didn't even know it had happened. I learned my youngest had been arrested from the Associated Press.

The circumstances of the arrest were thinner than they appeared in the press. The Glastonbury police stopped four kids in my car, found a single old roach under the backseat mat, and told Miki—without reading him his Miranda rights—that if he didn't claim it, all four would be arrested. He claimed it. It turned out later that the roach belonged to Cary, who was living in Japan at the time. But none of that mattered legally. Miki had said yes. And the system still treated him as a minor whose records deserved protection.

It hit the national news because I was head of the asset forfeiture unit in the U.S. Attorney's office in New Haven—the irony was too delicious for reporters to resist. I was removed from my position and transferred to the criminal division. The work itself was fine; I'd always loved criminal cases. But the scrutiny was relentless. For every court appearance of my son, the press was waiting outside.

Even then, even with my career derailed and my family exposed to public scrutiny, even with vindictive people trying to weaponize the legal system against me, due process worked. The investigation was thorough and fair. Miki's name was never formally broadcast—Ohta isn't a common name, and the press had already connected the dots—but his juvenile records were sealed, and the case was treated accordingly. My son was treated as a minor whose records deserved protection, not as a criminal whose identity could be broadcast.

When I got home that night, I told him I'd heard from the Associated Press. He said he didn't want to talk about it. I said okay, no problem. There wasn't anything else to say.

Iraqi children had none of that protection or leeway.

***

The trafficking reports made the disparity even more obvious. I read about a girl named Zeina in documents from the Organization of Women's Freedom in Iraq. She was thirteen when her grandfather sold her to a sex trafficker in Dubai for $6,000. For four years, she was forced into prostitution—oral sex with customers until a wealthy man paid $4,000 to take her virginity for one night.

When she was seventeen, Zeina managed to escape. She made her way back to Baghdad, back to her parents. She went to the authorities. She took her grandfather to court.

Then she disappeared.

The Organization of Women's Freedom in Iraq—a secular feminist human rights group that ran secret shelters for women and girls fleeing violence, honor killings, and trafficking—learned she'd been sold again, this time by her mother, to a sex trafficker in Erbil.

The girl had escaped. She'd sought help from the legal system. She'd done everything right. And her own mother sold her back into the same nightmare she'd just escaped.

That was what I was dealing with: a system where children were commodities, where family members were the traffickers, where even approaching the authorities for help offered no protection. The parents who should have protected these children were often complicit—sending them on criminal errands, selling them to traffickers, abandoning them to detention centers without legal representation.

I couldn't shake the unfairness of it. These children couldn't advocate for themselves. Their families weren't advocating for them—in many cases, the families were the ones exploiting them. The state that should have protected them sometimes criminalized them. And the international community that claimed to care about children's rights could only fund pilot programs and write reports while the machinery of injustice ground on.

***

In America, the system was built on different assumptions. Every juvenile facing charges had a right to legal representation. State agencies intervened when parents failed to protect their children. There were juvenile courts designed specifically to handle cases differently from adult criminal proceedings, recognizing that children's capacity for rehabilitation, culpability, and needs were different.

The American system wasn't perfect. State intervention could be excessive, even absurd. I'd seen cases during my career where overzealous child protection agencies removed children for infractions that seemed to violate common sense and parental rights. But even in those cases, even when the system overreached, every child had legal representation. Every parent had an attorney. Judges reviewed the decisions. There were appeals processes, oversight mechanisms, and legal standards that had to be met.

The U.S. system was built on a fundamental principle: children deserve protection and advocacy, and when their families fail them, the state has a responsibility to step in. But that state power had to be constrained by due process, by legal representation, and by judicial review.

I'd always believed the law should do what was right, not just what was minimally required. Early in my career, I learned about a case in Hawaii—a baby who suffered permanent brain damage during delivery due to clear medical malpractice at a U.S. government hospital. The mother never pursued her claim. By the time anyone told her what had actually happened, that it wasn't genetic, that it had occurred in the delivery room, the statute of limitations had run. The government had no legal liability. But Justice paid her anyway—thousands of dollars in compensation—because that child deserved it, whether the law required it or not. In private practice, you settle what you're required to settle and nothing more. That was never the kind of lawyer I wanted to be. The law should see the child, not just the liability.

I'd also learned that being tough didn't mean being heartless. As an assistant U.S. attorney defending civil cases brought against the government, plaintiffs on occasion actually complimented me for treating them fairly and with respect. They trusted me even when I was their adversary. I remembered a settlement conference before a U.S. magistrate years ago, a medical malpractice case involving a severely disabled child. The parents told the magistrate that they trusted me implicitly and would go along with whatever settlement amount I recommended. The magistrate nearly fell off his chair: "She's your adversary! You're not supposed to rely on the government's attorney!" The parents appreciated that I'd gone to the healthcare facility where their son lived, seen him in his highchair at roughly age six, and witnessed his reality. I was compassionate. I worked hard to be fair. You could be both tough and caring, aggressive and just.

The children in those Baghdad facilities had never encountered that combination. They had adults, often the parents, who used them as couriers or tools or commodities.

I'd seen vulnerable people throughout my career. In the Philippines with the Peace Corps, I'd encountered corruption and exploitation. In Bosnia, I'd worked in a war zone where institutional authority was fragile and contested. In various prosecutions, I'd dealt with victims who had no power and perpetrators who exploited that powerlessness.

But children were different. They were vulnerable in ways that adults, however disadvantaged, were not. They couldn't fully understand the systems acting on them. They couldn't navigate legal frameworks or advocate for their interests. They depended entirely on adults who were supposed to protect them—and when those adults failed them, when the state that should have stepped in instead criminalized them, they had nowhere to turn.

The UNICEF project aimed to develop vocational and educational programs, including literacy classes, social studies, business training, and introductory computer skills, to prepare children for eventual release and to provide advice on resources for employment, medical care, and social welfare.

Whether any of this would actually work remained an open question. The security situation prevented me from seeing the programs in action. The implementing partners submitted progress reports that I reviewed, looking for evidence that the money was being spent effectively, that the training was reaching the right people, and that children's conditions were actually improving.

But I couldn't shake a fundamental skepticism. We were trying to build a child welfare system in a country that had no cultural framework for seeing children as rights-bearing individuals. We were training judges in due process when due process itself was an imported concept that had never taken root. We were developing rehabilitation programs in a society that viewed children primarily as extensions of their families rather than as autonomous beings deserving independent protection.

The UNICEF project was another version of the same pattern: trying to establish children's rights within a system that had never recognized children's rights in the first place.

The project wasn't futile. The training mattered. The programs, if they were actually implemented, would help some children. The capacity-building might create lasting change among judges and prosecutors who genuinely wanted to reform the system.

But it was also a drop in an ocean of need. Twelve hundred boys and one hundred girls in detention facilities, each with a story of exploitation, abandonment, or simple bad luck of being born into circumstances where adults used them as tools. And beyond those thirteen hundred, countless others like Zeina who would cycle through systems of exploitation, who would face the same lack of protection and representation, who would discover that even escaping and seeking help offered no safety when their own families were the traffickers.

They weren't getting any of that. But I could document what I saw. I could insist on accuracy in reporting. I could push implementing partners to meet their obligations. I could refuse to let these children become invisible just because visiting their facilities was too dangerous, because acknowledging the full scope of their mistreatment was politically inconvenient, because American audiences wanted to hear stories of progress rather than accounts of ongoing failure.

The work was compromised, limited, and probably inadequate. I was representing American commitment to children's rights while America's own policy decisions—the war, the reconstruction, the eventual withdrawal—had created many of the conditions that put these children at risk in the first place. But it was what I could give them, so I did.

CHAPTER 11

THE SHELL GAME

The meetings were always held at the American Embassy compound. Twenty people from different countries would gather around a conference table—delegates from embassies and consulates across Baghdad—to discuss the trafficking statute Iraq still hadn't signed. The format was informal, almost collegial. *What's going on? What are you working on? How can we help each other?*

Everyone enjoyed coming. The compound was luxurious by Baghdad standards—the food, the swimming pool, the gyms. For diplomats stationed in this fractured city, an invitation to the American Embassy was a treat. We would discuss human trafficking while sitting in one of the safest and best-equipped compounds in Iraq, and then they'd go back to their respective postings to continue advocating for change.

I represented the United States, which held the biggest stick on paper. Congress had passed a statute saying the U.S. couldn't provide funds to any country that didn't prohibit human trafficking. It was our leverage. Ten years after the invasion, the Iraqis still hadn't passed the law. Ten years of meetings. Ten years of American money flowing anyway.

At first, no one around that table believed Congress would actually withdraw all funding. The leverage was the law. What it wasn't was real.

There was a doctrine in international law I'd thought about before I came to Iraq—the Responsibility to Protect. The principle is straightforward: if a government fails to protect its own people from atrocities, the international community has a responsibility to intervene. Not a right. A responsibility. But the doctrine had conditions. The intervention had to be collective, authorized through the UN, and undertaken only after peaceful measures were exhausted. And crucially, it didn't end with the intervention. The responsibility extended to the reconstruction—to building something legitimate in place of what had been destroyed.

We had invaded Iraq without that authorization, without exhausting alternatives, without a plan for what came after. I'd opposed the invasion on those grounds, not the ones most people cited. It wasn't just that the war was wrong—it was that we'd bypassed the very framework that would have given reconstruction its legitimacy. If the international community had intervened collectively, the rebuilding would have been a shared responsibility. Instead, it was ours alone—half-funded, politically contested, and apparently dependent on meetings where twenty diplomats ate our food, enjoyed our swimming pool, and went back to their embassies to watch the same laws go unenforced for another year.

That was the obligation we'd created for ourselves when we invaded. This was what meeting it looked like.

The working group itself was newer than the noncompliance it was trying to address. When I attended my first meeting in March 2011, it was only the group's second session. The delegates were still establishing basic "terms of reference"—what the group's mission actually was, what its role in the legislative process would be, and how it would collect and assess existing data. They were writing a statement of work for a coalition that had not yet defined its own purpose. Ten years of American leverage. Ten years of Iraqi noncompliance. And the multinational response was still introducing itself.

It was inexplicable. They'd signed other international documents that they never followed. So why not sign this one, too? They could put their names on the paper and then do nothing about it, just like everything else. That's what I couldn't understand. It's not like they were going to enforce it.

The leverage traced back to 2000 when the United Nations adopted the Palermo Protocol—the first international instrument with an agreed definition of human trafficking. It called for criminalizing all acts of trafficking and established what they called the "3P" paradigm: prevention, criminal prosecution, and victim protection. The same year, Congress enacted the Trafficking Victims Protection Act, which gave teeth to the protocol by threatening to withhold funding from noncompliant countries.

What shocked me, once I started reading the State Department Reports on Human Trafficking, was learning that trafficking wasn't just an Iraqi problem. The reports were published annually for almost every country—lengthy documents, almost like legal briefs, with statistics people relied on for policy decisions. And relatively recently, the State Department started publishing one for the United States. I'd never thought human trafficking was a serious problem in our country. The problem wasn't geography. It was enforcement.

Eventually, Iraq passed it. But even the law itself had a hole cut into it. It criminalized labor trafficking and most forms of sex trafficking—up to life imprisonment for offenses involving women and children. On paper, the penalties were stringent. But it required a demonstration of force, fraud, or coercion to constitute a child sex trafficking offense, which meant it didn't criminalize all forms of child sex trafficking. A grandfather selling his granddaughter to a trafficker in Dubai—if he hadn't used force, fraud, or coercion, if she had simply complied out of fear, ignorance, or dependency—the law might not reach him at all. They'd signed the paper. They'd written the loophole into the paper at the same time.

The Iraqis knew it too. A senior Iraqi deputy minister said it on the record: "I admit that Iraqi government institutions are not mature enough to deal with this topic yet, as the departments are still in their growing phase."

Human Rights Watch was blunter. The government hadn't monitored traffickers, hadn't cracked down on them, and, because of that, they said, there was "a black hole in terms of information." No data. No enforcement. No consequences.

And the counter-trafficking law that might have changed that had been stalled in the Iraqi government since 2009—two years before I arrived, and still going nowhere when I left.

What made it worse was who bore the cost. It wasn't the traffickers. Perversely, it was often the victims of trafficking and prostitution who were punished. The grandfather who sold Zeina walked free while she disappeared into another trafficker's hands. The brothel operator known as Emam—whose ties to the Interior Ministry were an open secret in Baghdad—had never had a single house shut down despite years of public exposure. The system wasn't simply failing to prosecute traffickers. In many cases, it was protecting them.

***

The Peace Corps had prepared me for this in ways I hadn't fully appreciated at the time. In the Philippines, I was surrounded by what looked like corruption on a regular basis—but it wasn't always the kind you could prosecute.

I've mentioned the housekeeper who took my roommate's blouse, among other items. What I didn't describe was visiting her home.

She lived in a squatter's field, a little elevated shack with no furniture except two stools her family had made specially for us to sit on. She'd bought canned pineapple juice and a loaf of white bread to honor us—items she'd never have purchased for herself. And she was wearing my roommate's blouse and her earrings. Greeting cards we had thrown away were displayed on her walls, along with wrapping paper, smoothed out and hung like art. No shame. No embarrassment. She didn't think she'd done anything wrong.

When our cottage was broken into while we were away, the thieves took one of our two Peace Corps-issued bicycles but not the other. One radio but not the other. My guitar, but not my ukulele. Half the food in the refrigerator, all of the jewelry in my roommate's drawer, but none of mine.

Initially, our neighbors thought we were selfish because we played our radio at a low volume (out of courtesy) rather than loud enough for everyone to enjoy. In their moral framework, we learned we were being selfish for not sharing, so we turned up the volume.

Corruption has a specific legal meaning: bribery, kickbacks, money changing hands. But what I learned in the Philippines was something different—a world where the rules themselves were understood differently, where taking what you needed from people who had more wasn't "theft" but redistribution, where sharing wasn't optional but obligatory. At one point, I saw in the open-air market one of the blue radios issued to each volunteer with the notice, in large letters, "Property of the U.S. Peace Corps." No effort was made to obliterate the notice. I wondered if it was the one taken from us.

***

In Iraq, I saw non-compliance with international protocols that the government had signed. Children in detention facilities that violated the standards Iraq had agreed to meet. Trafficking laws that existed on paper but meant little in practice. It wasn't corruption in the cash-in-pocket sense; it was something harder to prosecute: the gap between what a country promises and what it actually does.

I'd been prepared for that gap; I just hadn't expected it to feel so familiar.

I was an "in the weeds" kind of litigator. I liked concrete milestones—going to trial, completing tasks with measurable outcomes. In Iraq, there were no concrete measures of success or failure. The concepts were amorphous, ephemeral, pie-in-the-sky ideals. You couldn't tell how much difference you were making because you probably weren't making any.

The system didn't want truth—the suppressed detention report had already taught me that. They wanted favorable optics, not facts.

I knew what accountability looked like. I'd spent my career in rooms where the games had consequences.

***

The Black Hawk helicopter case was one of the biggest criminal matters the Connecticut U.S. Attorney's Office had ever handled. A friend of mine had sat on it for nearly four years—boxes stacked in the corner of his office, untouched. The case was extraordinarily complicated, just numbers and audit trails, dry as dust. When they asked me to take it over, I had only six months before the statute of limitations ran out.

The government procures equipment in two ways: fixed-price contracts and time-and-materials contracts. Each Black Hawk helicopter was a separate fixed-price contract. The rules forbade transferring materials from one helicopter's production line to another. For example, if one assembly ran short of a specific part, the contractor was not allowed to "borrow" the part from another production line.

The violation was buried at the thirteenth or fourteenth level of Sikorsky's documents, which requested payment for each individual helicopter as it came off the assembly line. The Defense Contract Audit Agency (DCAA) had auditors stationed full-time at the Sikorsky facility, but they focused their scrutiny on time-and-materials contracts, where billing fraud was easier to commit and detect. Fixed-price contracts received less attention. The government paid the agreed amount, got its helicopter, and that was the end of the story. The DCAA auditors had no reason to dig deep enough to catch material transfers between production lines, which would reveal this type of fraud.

But someone inside the company knew. The vice president of finance, for reasons that were not clear to me, wore a hidden body mic to an internal meeting where in-house attorneys and lawyers from D.C. discussed audit issues. He secretly recorded everything. On the tape, one could hear them saying words to the effect: "DCAA will never find out because they never audit to that depth. It's fixed price. They got the helicopter; we got paid. What's the big deal?"

The big deal was that Sikorsky was breaking the law every time they submitted an improper invoice. The harm to the government was the time value of the money.

The vice president of finance retained a well-known Connecticut attorney, and they filed a "qui tam" action, commonly known as a whistleblower complaint, with notice to the government. The Justice Department then took over the litigation and turned the case over to the U.S. Attorney's Office in Connecticut. A team was assembled: two special agents from each of four different agencies, eight people working frantically while I tried to understand what we were dealing with.

I was desperate. The statute of limitations was running, and there was no way to extend it. I had the tapes transcribed and spent every available moment studying them. One holiday weekend, I drove from New Haven to my niece's house with the car windows closed and no air conditioning. I had headphones on, listening to the recordings. I fell asleep at the wheel on I-95, hit the guardrail, spun around, and hit the guardrail on the other side. My little Geo bounced between the barriers like a pinball. The cars behind me must have seen my head nodding—they'd already stopped. Somehow, I managed to drive to my destination in a rather battered car.

That's how driven I was.

The settlement negotiations were held in the main conference room in the DOJ-leased space in New Haven. I sat at the head of the table with my pile of files. The eight agents sat in the back of the room. And then there were the defense attorneys—the local counsel who'd been dealing with me for months, the D.C. lawyers, and a new addition: a partner from Wachtell Lipton in New York. I later learned his salary was $850,000 a year. The treasurer of United Technologies, Sikorsky's parent company, was there too.

The tapes were a huge issue. The defense claimed attorney-client privilege—there'd been maybe ten lawyers at that internal meeting. I looked at the new attorney from New York, the one who'd just arrived to take over the case.

"Will you waive the privilege?" I asked. "Because you're talking about committing fraud on those recordings."

He said they were going to take it to the judge.

And then he got sleazy. Something in his manner shifted, that particular arrogance of a man who bills more per hour than I made in a week.

"Excuse me, sir," I said. "Are you threatening to have me disqualified for listening to those tapes?"

"Yes," he said. "I am."

I closed my folders. I stood up. "Gentlemen, this meeting is hereby terminated. Have a nice trip back to D.C."

My agents in the back of the room nearly had heart attacks. "Leslie, you can't just walk away—this is the biggest case we've ever had in Connecticut."

But I didn't care. The New York attorney said he was going straight to the U.S. Attorney.

"Be my guest," I said. "The elevator's right there. Go down one floor."

The other defense attorneys—the ones who'd been working with me for months, who knew how I operated—started trying to calm him down. And then they fired him. Right there in the room. "You're not representing us any longer."

They knew perfectly well that if I were disqualified, the case would be over. The statute of limitations was running. No other attorney could take over in time. And they weren't going to get an extension.

The government settled both the civil and criminal cases for $3.5 million—the largest settlement of its kind at the time. The time value of money, mostly. Progress payments the government had made too early, interest on funds that should have stayed in our accounts. My office was convinced that my aggressive stance forced United Technologies to the table. I got all kinds of accolades.

Can you imagine me in private practice? I wouldn't have lasted a week. But that was why I stayed at Justice for my entire career, at relatively low pay considering my credentials. You had that autonomy. You had that integrity. I could do things like that, and my office would support me. We didn't represent people. We didn't represent agencies. We represented the United States.

***

Sitting at those coalition roundtables in Baghdad, I thought about that conference room in Connecticut. Twenty people around a table there too. But in Connecticut, someone had worn a wire. Someone had called the bluff. Someone had paid three and a half million dollars because the alternative was worse. The rules had meant something. I had meant something.

In Baghdad, I represented the United States at a table where everyone understood the money would flow regardless. The rules were theater. And some days, I wondered if I was, too.

Eventually, Congress got fed up. They passed their statute prohibiting funds to countries that didn't have anti-trafficking laws. That was the leverage. Finally, Iraq signed the legislation.

And then, as far as I know, they didn't do anything.

All Congress wanted was the signature. Make it the law so they could feel better. There was nothing about proving enforcement. How could there be? It was just theater. The statute would pass, the money would flow, and the trafficking would continue in the shadows.

I've always believed people should do things because they think it's right, not because someone's holding money over their head. But I wasn't writing the statute.

And sometimes the law didn't even pretend to matter.

***

That July, Muqtada al-Sadr's movement won pardons for at least fifty prisoners: murderers, kidnappers, and men convicted of attacks on American troops. Some had been sentenced under anti-terrorism laws, which the Iraqi Constitution specifically forbade pardoning. But Prime Minister Maliki needed Sadr's backing to stay in power. Sadr was a useful man to need—a cleric who publicly positioned himself as a reformer fighting corruption while simultaneously running what amounted to a state within a state, his armed militia operating alongside the official security apparatus, and his political movement engineering amnesties for followers the judiciary had managed to convict.

The Parliament Speaker saw what was happening. "The credibility of the judiciary will be gone," he warned, "especially when it comes to terrorist cases."

We were teaching police officers to gather evidence, build cases, and follow procedures. And the Prime Minister was releasing convicted terrorists to keep his coalition together. The judicial process was subjected to political negotiation. The rights of victims were sacrificed.

I thought about the children in Iraq's detention facilities—held for months, sometimes years, on insufficient evidence, with no attorneys and no path out. The system that couldn't move to release them could move very efficiently when Sadr needed it to.

The same pattern played out with female genital mutilation. I was part of a coalition working on FGM legislation, and Iraq actually passed the law. It felt like a victory—a concrete accomplishment in a place where victories were rare. But I knew what would happen next. The law would exist in Baghdad, but the practice would continue in the villages. They'd passed a statute, but the villages were still going to do it.

Iraq had passed the statute to get American money, but they weren't enforcing it. The Court recognized the shell game.

"I will see you tomorrow, *Inshallah*." "We will sign the contract tomorrow, *Inshallah*." "We will work together, *Inshallah*." Never "I will do it." Never "I will be there." Even when there wasn't a snowball's chance in hell of something happening, it was still *Inshallah*.

For the first few months, I found that word charming. I started using it myself when speaking to Iraqis. Now I understood it differently.

Whenever I experienced a setback on one of my projects—which happened far too often—I'd take a deep breath and tell myself to accept it. Whatever will be, will be. I can't make things happen. I must be resigned to the inevitable.

I'd become the personification of *Inshallah*. My lack of accomplishments must be God's will. I wasn't responsible.

It was a survival mechanism, not a philosophy. But the line between the two had blurred. Even my appointment at the beauty shop, it turned out, had needed the word.

But *Inshallah* was never going to be enough for me. Even when the evidence said otherwise, I needed to believe I could affect outcome. So I looked for places where I still could.

***

In September, we hosted Iraqi Girls Spa Day at the Embassy—an event organized by American staff for the daughters and nieces of local employees. We followed it up in November with Boys Fun Day. I volunteered to be one of two team leaders. There was a lot of work getting ready and a lot of work cleaning up. But the event was a tremendous boost to our emotional well-being.

We set up stations in the lobby of one of the apartment buildings where the kids made tie-dyed and painted T-shirts. Then we transported them to the swimming pool—and it was hard to get them out until we told them the next stop was the fire station. They got to wear the firemen's gear. They got to try knocking a plastic bottle off a cone with a fire hose. I tried too and failed.

We played games on the green: sack races, three-legged races, and an obstacle course. The kids ran and laughed and competed the way kids do everywhere.

Many of the adults who came—mostly fathers and uncles—said it was the best day in the lives of the children.

Later, I organized an art show—Iraqi artists displaying their work inside the embassy walls. Another success. I still have some of the pieces hanging in my house.

I loved planning these events. Everyone thought they were wonderful. And they were.

But I understood what they were. Girls' Day, Boys' Day, the art show—these were goodwill gestures. Feel-good diplomacy. It would be nice if the Iraqis liked us, but it didn't really matter whether they did. We were going to be there regardless. They had no choice in the arrangement.

I'm proud of both kinds of work. But I know the difference.

***

The Department of Justice had sent experts to help write Iraq's new constitution. So had other European countries. The document they produced was, in many ways, superior to our own—it guaranteed healthcare and protected women's rights in ways the American Constitution doesn't. On paper, it was a paradigm.

But a constitution is just paper if no one enforces it. A trafficking statute is just words if the money flows anyway. An FGM law is just theater if the villages keep cutting.

The shell game was the system itself. Everyone knew the shells were empty. The money flowed anyway. The meetings continued. The roundtables convened. The reports were filed.

Inshallah.

CHAPTER 12

FACING THE INTERNATIONAL ROUNDS

Of everything I did in Iraq—the prison visits, the police training, the constitutional discussions, the coalition meetings that went nowhere—the Jessup Moot Court competition was where I felt I'd made the most difference. It was the highlight of my year, and the international rounds in Washington were its finale.

I flew home in early March, stopped briefly in Germany to see Miki and my grandchildren, then continued to Connecticut before heading to Washington. The Iraqi teams would arrive on March 25. I had less than two weeks to prepare. I would not be participating as a Commercial Litigation Branch Attorney but as part of my detail with OPDAT, part of the Criminal Branch.

The visa situation had consumed my final weeks in Iraq. I'd been at the embassy visa office practically every day, watching the clock run down. All five women from Baghdad College of Law received approval, as did their dean. However, Dr. Hadi, the team advisor who'd worked with them for months, wasn't granted a visa in time. Three members of the Thi-Qar team weren't granted visas either.

The problem, I learned, was their names. Muhammad. Hassan. These are among the most common names in the Arab world—there are millions of men with these names, spelled many different ways. The embassy staff in D.C. tried their best to track down exactly which Muhammad, which Hassan, but they couldn't do so in time. The women's names were more unique, easier to verify. The system wasn't being arbitrary; it was being overwhelmed by the impossibility of identifying specific individuals when so many shared the same names.

That didn't make it any less devastating for the men who couldn't come.

The final traveling group consisted of the dean from Baghdad College of Law and all five of the women's team members, plus the dean from Thi-Qar, their team advisor, and only two of their original team members. Baghdad College of Law would formally represent Iraq in the competition; Thi-Qar, having lost three of its five members to the visa problem, would compete as an exhibition team. Three staff members from Access to Justice would accompany them, along with Connie Bowden, the recently retired Assistant U.S. Attorney from Pittsburgh who'd done two details in Iraq and had volunteered to help me shepherd the students through their ten-day stay.

I'd booked rooms for everyone at the Capital Hilton, the competition venue. About 130 teams from 80 countries would participate—a truly global gathering of law students, all arguing variations of the same hypothetical international law problem before panels of judges from around the world.

When the Iraqi students arrived, I watched their faces as they took in Washington for the first time. These young women had spent months preparing legal arguments in a war zone, had won their country's national competition, and had navigated a visa process that had excluded some of their colleagues. Now they were walking through the lobby of a Washington hotel, surrounded by law students from Moscow, London, Beijing, and Bogotá.

These weren't just law students; they were Iraq's legal future. In ten years, twenty years, they would be judges, prosecutors, human rights lawyers, and legal scholars who would shape their country's institutions. They would remember this week in Washington.

***

The competition itself lasted three days. Each team argued for four rounds, switching between representing the applicant nation and the respondent nation, demonstrating they could argue either side of the hypothetical dispute with equal facility. The Baghdad team had decided to argue in Arabic—their English was good enough for presentations but not for the rapid-fire judicial questioning that defined moot court competition. Interpreters translated throughout.

They faced King's College London in the first round, then Peking University, and then law schools from Croatia and Belgium. Four rounds against teams from countries with established legal education systems, with students who'd grown up in peacetime, who'd never had to duck into bunkers during mortar attacks or wonder if their team advisor would be granted a visa.

On the third day, the top thirty-two teams were announced in the evening. Baghdad College of Law had lost all four rounds. They did not advance. Moscow State would go on to face Columbia in the finals. Moscow would win. One of Columbia's oralists would receive the Best Oralist Award. The Iraqi women would go home without a trophy.

But the scoreboard didn't capture what they'd actually accomplished. I'd known that from the beginning—the competition was never really the point.

***

Showing people new worlds was something I'd always loved. Two months after my wedding to Toshi, my father came to Japan—he hadn't attended the lavish Shinto ceremony, and afterward, I planned a trip for just the two of us through Southeast Asia. I booked five-star hotels the whole way.

My father was a humble man. When we arrived in Hong Kong, a uniformed chauffeur met us at the airport. "Welcome to Hong Kong, Mr. Cayer and Mrs. Ohta." His eyes went wide. They took us to the Peninsula, and the next morning, porters at every intersection greeted us by name. He couldn't believe it.

In Bali, I'd hired a car and driver. We were passing through the countryside when we came upon a huge field filled with hundreds of people in small clusters, all digging. I asked the driver to stop.

"Oh yes," he said. "They're digging up the corpses of their family members. You can only properly dispose of them every fifty years, and today is the day."

They'd unearth the bones, wrap them, paint faces on the shrouds, build little platforms on stilts, and set them on fire. My father was horrified. "This is so invasive. We shouldn't be watching."

"They don't mind," I told him. "Everyone's doing it. No one cares that we're here."

Then—I don't even remember how—I met a member of the Balinese royal family. Someone in his family had just died, and he invited us to the wake at his home. Afterward, they carried the body out on a tiered platform to the middle of a field. People stood in a circle holding palm fronds with writing on them, lit them on fire, and watched them float upward. They built a pyre and set it ablaze. You could see the body fall through the bottom.

My father finally understood. The royal family member hadn't just tolerated our presence—he'd opened his door and said, "This is for you too." That was the invitation that made the difference. Not the observation from the road, but being brought inside.

That was what I was doing in Washington.

***

The competition was only part of what we'd planned for their ten days in Washington. I'd arranged activities to show them what American legal institutions looked like and what democratic governance felt like when it was functioning.

We toured the Supreme Court—a private tour arranged through contacts I'd cultivated over thirty years at the Justice Department. The students stood in the chamber where *Brown v. Board of Education* had been decided, where *Roe v. Wade* had been argued, where the fundamental questions of American constitutional law had been debated and resolved. They asked questions about judicial independence, about lifetime appointments, and about how the Court maintained its authority when it had no army to enforce its decisions.

We visited the Court of Federal Claims, where Chief Judge Hewitt gave a talk about specialized courts and demonstrated the electronic capabilities of a modern American courtroom. They peppered him with questions about evidence, procedure, and the mechanics of litigation in a system where technology and tradition intersected.

We went to USAID, the agency that had sponsored their trip. We visited the Iraqi Embassy, where they could speak Arabic and, for a moment, feel like they were home. We toured GW Law School, where American students and faculty described their own moot court program, and the young women could see what legal education looked like in peacetime.

One evening, I arranged dinner with the teams from Afghanistan and Palestine. Three countries, three very different conflicts, three groups of law students who understood something about practicing law in impossible circumstances. They talked late into the night—in English, in Arabic, in whatever common language they could find—about justice and governance and what it meant to build legal institutions when everything around you was uncertain. They had found each other.

I felt what I always feel when I show someone a world they haven't seen before.

***

On Sunday, we celebrated the birthday of one of the Baghdad students with brunch at Washington Harbor. Then, while shopping at Pentagon City, the young women were fascinated by American consumer culture, by the sheer abundance of everything, by the normalcy of it all.

I've never taken an interest in shiny, expensive things—not the way these girls seemed to. Early in our marriage, someone from Toshi's family sent him $18,000 to buy us Christmas presents. This was forty years ago; it was a lot of money.

Toshi bought two Rolex watches. Toshi's cost $14,000; mine, $4,000.

I wasn't even into watches. I'm not into jewelry. I'd never spend more than $200 on a watch. But I wore it—wore it all the time—doing housework, yard work, and painting the fence.

Toshi had a jeweler he visited every three months to have his Rolex cleaned. He'd bring mine in less often, but occasionally. After a year or two, the jeweler—I'd never even met the man—said to Toshi, "I don't know your wife. I don't hate your wife. But I will not clean her watch anymore. She has no respect for it. This is disgraceful. There's paint, there's grass, there's dirt, scratches everywhere. This is no way to treat a Rolex."

He cleaned it the last time. Then we went down to North Carolina to visit our son and his wife—she's a doctor—and Toshi gave her the watch. I was happy to see it go.

***

The team and I later walked the National Mall, visited the monuments, stood before the Lincoln Memorial, and talked about the Civil War, Reconstruction, and what it takes to rebuild a nation. We stopped at the White House, too—they stood at the fence and looked at it for a long time without saying much.

I'd wanted to do the same for Sarah.

She wasn't in Washington for the moot court—she was finishing her residency in Baghdad. But I'd helped her with a visa application months earlier, prepared a detailed itinerary, and made the case that this Iraqi doctor who'd risked everything by working with Americans deserved to see the country she'd been serving. The visa was granted. I had plans: Disney World with my sister Marilyn and Connie; the train to New York City with my nieces, Nikki and Caroline. I wanted her to see as much as possible.

Three days before we were supposed to leave, her brother was seriously injured in a car accident. Sarah canceled. Of course she did.

I never got to show her America. But Sarah found her own new world: a master's program at the American University in Beirut—$30,000, funded in part by connections she'd made through the PRT. Then, a cardiothoracic surgery program in England. The last I heard, she was thriving there—practicing medicine at the highest level in a country where she didn't have to hide who she was or calculate whom she could trust with what she really did. We're still in touch, mostly through Facebook—sharing professional accomplishments and photos of an ordinary life. The kind of peace she couldn't have had in Baghdad.

She didn't need me to show her the door. She walked through it herself.

***

When I watched the law students board the plane back to Baghdad, one of the young women hugged me and said this had been the most important experience of her life. I believed her. I'm not given to sentiment, but I stood at that gate longer than I needed to.

They'd lost every round of the competition. But they'd represented Iraq on an international stage. They'd seen what American institutions looked like, had asked hard questions, and had connected with students from other countries facing their own impossible situations. These young women would go home changed, and they would change their country.

I'd taken something that was about to collapse when DePaul Law School abandoned the project, and I'd made it work. I'd gotten Iraqi law students to Washington. I'd watched them argue international law before judges from around the world. I'd seen them energized by the experience. That was why this mattered more to me than anything else I'd done in Iraq. This was concrete. This was visible.

The thing I'd wanted most—a women's legal clinic, a place where Iraqi women could actually access the legal system—I never even got it off the ground. The circumstances swallowed it. Everything else I'd done in Iraq had been compromised in some way: the shell game of trafficking legislation, the bulldozed crime scene, the children prosecuted for crimes that adults had made them commit, the institutions that looked good on paper but crumbled in practice.

That was what I wanted to believe the work had meant. Not the failures, but the seeds. Not the institutions that couldn't hold, but the individuals who would carry something forward. This was the part that worked.

CHAPTER 13

THE STOREROOM WELCOME

Weeks before I was scheduled to leave Iraq, I sent an email to my office in the Commercial Litigation Branch. I informed them I'd return on Monday, March 9. I had been requested by DePaul College of Law, the organizers of the Jessup Moot Court Competition, to score memorials, given my familiarity with the factual and legal issues. I requested permission to spend my first week back scoring memorials for the Jessup International Rounds and the second week assisting the two Iraqi teams during their nine-day visit to Washington.

I construed the lack of a timely response as tacit approval. I notified the International Law Students Association that I'd be a scoring judge for ten memorials. I advised OPDAT and USAID that I'd assist the Iraqi teams. The logistics were in place.

Then, shortly before I was scheduled to leave Iraq, I received an email from the Deputy Director. The Branch Director wanted a "memorandum" regarding my requests—

no explanation of what additional information she needed beyond what I'd already provided. I sent the memorandum anyway.

The response came as a copy of an email from the Director to the Deputy Director: I could not be out of the office for two weeks. If I wanted to continue working on the Jessup competition, I'd have to take two weeks of annual leave or leave without pay.

I gave the Director the benefit of the doubt. Maybe there were urgent cases waiting. Maybe my full-time efforts would be required immediately. On several occasions, significant cases had been reassigned to me for various reasons. Perhaps the press of work genuinely demanded my attention.

I also understood that my going hadn't been universally welcomed. I was the first attorney from the Commercial Litigation Branch to volunteer for Iraq. When I left, my cases had to be redistributed—no one had been hired to cover them, and no one had been detailed in. Management apparently hadn't wanted their attorneys getting ideas about adventure elsewhere, and a year-long absence was an inconvenience the Branch had absorbed without enthusiasm. That history didn't disappear when I stepped off the plane.

I notified the ILSA that I couldn't fulfill my commitment to score the memorials. The Iraqi teams were another matter. OPDAT and USAID were counting on me to be there for the students' nine-day visit, and I intended to honor that commitment on my own time, using annual leave if necessary. That much wasn't the Director's to take away.

On a Monday in March, after brief stops in Germany and Connecticut, I took the elevator up to my office. I didn't expect a welcome committee. But when I opened the door, I found my office had been used as a storage room. Boxes everywhere. Chairs stacked against the walls. I had to move furniture just to reach my desk. I was surprised. And offended. And, if I'm honest, outraged.

There was nothing on my desk. I checked the mail room—nothing there either. No cases had been assigned to me.

By Friday of my first week, I still hadn't been assigned any cases. By Thursday of the second week—nothing.

I stood at that empty desk and took stock. Thirty-two years of federal service. Nearly as long as my marriage. The Attorney General's Honors Program. Sixty trials as lead counsel. Hundreds of appeals. Prosecutor of the Year from the Connecticut Association of Chiefs of Police. The Milton S. Camilleri Distinguished Service Award. Heading the Asset Forfeiture Unit for the entire state of Connecticut. The A-12 stealth airplane litigation—a multi-billion-dollar contract dispute where I'd been responsible for presenting evidence on stealth technology and the aircraft's propulsion system. A year in the Office of Immigration Litigation, writing briefs and arguing asylum cases, learning exactly how much the courts relied on State Department human rights reports. Election monitoring in Bosnia, where I'd investigated voter registration fraud and helped get an unjustly fired official reinstated. Top seven percent of my law school class. Tied for the highest score with one other on the Connecticut State bar exam. Publishing in the Law Review as a first-year student—an achievement that had seemed impossible for someone who'd entered law school at thirty-seven, uncertain whether she belonged there at all.

Whatever goodwill I'd carried back from Iraq was gone. It wasn't the pressure of urgent cases that had prevented me from acting as a scoring judge. There were no urgent cases. There were no cases at all.

The next Thursday morning, I went to the Deputy Director's office. "If the Director is not willing to change her mind and authorize me to spend next week assisting the Iraqi Moot Court teams during the International Rounds," I said, "then Friday will be my last day."

The Director did not blink. Neither did I.

***

There's one story I find funny now. We were in the States, Cary maybe four years old, Miki around two. Toshi was out with his mistress, and somehow, I knew where they were. So I drove to the restaurant and saw his car. I said, "Cary, let's play the snake game." I showed him how to push the valve on the tire—it makes a hissing sound. We let the air out of all of Toshi's tires. That's probably the only overt thing I ever did. I don't think Toshi ever suspected I would have done that, or could have.

That's about the size of my appetite for revenge.

I understood what this was. I'd spent enough years in Japan to recognize institutional indifference—and to distinguish it from personal betrayal. I knew how to read unspoken signals, how to understand shame culture and face-saving protocols, how to tell the difference between genuine threat and mere thoughtlessness.

During law school, I was studying twelve hours a day, which meant Toshi had to manage the kids. One Sunday, he came to me and said, "I can't do this anymore."

So I said, "That's fine. I'll quit. When the kids are both in school full-time, I'll go back."

I knew enough about Japanese culture to know exactly what would happen next. He apologized profusely, said he would never bring the subject up again. For me to quit law school would be a huge disgrace in Japan—and we both understood this, even though we didn't live there anymore, even though he had no connection with his family, even though no one in America would criticize a woman for leaving law school for a couple of years until her children were school-aged.

He never complained again after that.

Toshi "betrayed" me on numerous occasions—or would have, by American standards. Probably the worst was when one of his mistresses rang our apartment doorbell in Japan. I can't remember if we had our first child yet. That was so against Japanese culture. Mistresses know they're mistresses. To invade the privacy of our home was the betrayal—not the affair itself. Toshi answered the door, she left, and she never came back. I'm sure Toshi ended the affair with her. She'd acted outside the cultural norms.

I didn't feel threatened; I didn't get my feelings hurt. He picked me. I was his choice. And he'd given up a lot for marrying me—certainly monetarily. To go from a thirty-room mansion to a three-room apartment.

But here's what Japan also taught me: you don't have to accept every framework you understand.

***

When I stood in that Justice Department hallway, looking at the storage room that used to be my office, I didn't feel betrayed. The Director's refusal to let me help with Jessup wasn't personal. This may simply have been an example of randomness or capriciousness. The empty desk, the missing cases, the bureaucratic indifference—none of it was about me or my worthiness. It was an institution that had forgotten how to value its people.

I'd seen this before. In the stealth airplane case, one of my key expert witnesses was a young Egyptian man—brilliant in computer modeling, ten years in the country, PhD earned here, and a career built here. We'd paid him a million dollars to build a CAD model of the aircraft. The Navy needed his testimony.

Then a routine blood test turned up undiagnosed HIV. By law, that meant immediate deportation. The rule was absolute. He had no symptoms, no idea he was infected. It didn't matter.

Except we needed him. And suddenly, the rule had a waiver. DOJ took a stand. The Navy took a stand. The young man stayed, completed his work, and helped us win the case.

The institution bent its own rules when the institution needed them bent. It didn't bend them for me. It didn't bend them for the Iraqi law students.

I understood how this worked.

***

Wednesday, I went down to personnel. "I'm done."

"You need to give six weeks' notice."

"No. Friday is my last day."

Everybody knew me, and they were shocked.

The most amazing part was how content I was with my decision. I'd expected that retiring would be traumatic, depressing—I'd always loved my work. Instead, I felt privileged to be able to state unequivocally that I never wrote or argued anything in court that I didn't passionately believe. I also felt something close to relief. I needed that proverbial kick in the pants to make the decision. For that, I was grateful to the Director.

I walked out of the Justice Department building for the last time. There were new rivers to ford, new mountains to climb. I couldn't wait to get started.

CHAPTER 14

MY FATHER'S DAUGHTER

My father was a really exceptional person. I say that not because he basically raised three children alone after my mother died, though he did.

Funny, I remember the wake very well. My mother was wearing a blue suit, a gold lapel watch, and glasses. I thought it was the weirdest thing—putting glasses on a dead person. But apparently, that's how people remember you. The casket was lined with yellow satin. I'd known she was gone before anyone told me. A day or two after the only visit the hospital allowed my brother, sister, and me, I walked in from the garage and found her rose-colored bathrobe and a jar of colored sour balls on the workbench in the basement. These items had been on her hospital bedside table. Nobody ever said, "Your mother died." I just knew.

Some of them criticized my father for having all of us children there. He didn't care. That was my father—he had his own ideas about what was right, and he raised us the same way.

For a while after, I would dream about walking down Main Street in Hartford. My dad used to bring us to G. Fox for shopping and lunch. And I would think: *someday I'm going to see my mom walking down the street.* I knew it wasn't true. But I wanted to believe it was possible.

Years later, I took my boys to see *E.T.* I started crying. Miki was maybe five years old. He said, "Mom, you don't have to cry. It's not real."

I told him, "You can't be sure of that. It could be real."

Whenever I got in trouble at school—and I got in trouble often—my father would make me sit down across the table from him. No yelling, no hitting. Just: blah, blah, blah, blah, blah. Sometimes I wanted to say, "Why don't you just punish me and get it over with?" Because I knew what was coming. He would talk about consequences. About choices. Not with anger, just with this patient, relentless logic. If you do this, then this will happen. If those consequences are acceptable to you, then proceed.

He supported my instincts and value system. Which made his feelings about lawyers all the more...challenging.

To my father, lawyers were people who said whatever they were paid to say. Hired guns without conviction. Why would someone with integrity choose a profession built on arguing positions you don't believe? It was, however, not a subject we discussed. My interest was in science and math.

I didn't become a lawyer until I was thirty-seven, after the Peace Corps, after Japan, after teaching English, working in movies, and raising two children. When I told him I'd been accepted to law school, he was supportive.

But did I prove my father wrong about lawyers? Yes. Definitely. He knew I always took the high road.

Three times in my career, I was asked to take a position I believed was wrong. Three times, I went to my supervisor and refused. Those three times matter to me more than I can express—not because I wanted to be difficult, but because I couldn't argue something I knew to be false or ill-advised. Each time, when I explained my reasoning, my supervisor agreed with my analysis. The law, I discovered, was about seeking truth—not obscuring it.

The same principle followed me out of the courtroom. After Iraq, back in Connecticut, I ran for Town Council in Glastonbury—six months after I'd moved there, with no name recognition whatsoever. I had to join the Democratic Party to get on the ballot, which didn't stop me from telling voters I was pro-military, pro-law enforcement, fiscally conservative, and a social justice advocate. I lost by eighteen votes. I could have had a recount; I didn't ask for one.

What I admire about the military is the discipline, the training, and the commitment to a higher ideal. Staying in your lane—not that I always stayed in mine, but I have great respect for it. Same with law enforcement.

If my father had lived to see Iraq, he would have been proud of me. I know this in my bones—not because I succeeded; no one was going to in a single deployment—but because I showed up and did the work, without flinching and without compromise. I was willing to take the risks. I hoped I could make a difference in a country where we'd caused so much pain, a country I felt strongly we should never have invaded in the first place.

I think it's important to take risks—to try something you might not succeed at. Americans are so obsessed with failure. Some may not take a course because they fear they will not ace it. But you can learn from your failures. You can learn from your mistakes—sometimes more than you learn from success.

My father knew better than anyone: when I make up my mind, I make up my mind. He'd seen it with Toshi, too.

***

Toshi still comes to the house two or three times a week, mainly for the dog, our son, and the grandkids, but we chat.

He walks into a house full of Japan—woodblock prints, swords, and artifacts from decades of collecting. In the kitchen, with its cathedral ceilings, one whole wall is covered with hats from the Philippines. Every village has its own style—different shapes, different materials, not all conical as you might think. I collected them during my time in the Peace Corps. Stuff from all over the world, really—forty-eight countries' worth. Art from the show we hosted at the embassy, which I'm especially proud of.

Toshi's townhouse has none of this. Exquisite taste in furniture, impeccable clothes—he still pays two thousand dollars for a coat—but very few items from Japan. I'm the one who holds onto the heritage.

Some American friends find our relationship incomprehensible. We've been divorced for years. He has a girlfriend who's been with him for two decades now—she comes to the Japanese New Year's party, and she once came with us to

Rocking Horse Ranch with her daughter. But she doesn't live with him. I doubt he'll ever marry her. In Japan, there's a clear distinction between a wife and a mistress. Once a mistress, always a mistress.

We still share a life in practical ways—birthdays, taxes, the occasional favor.

What's the difference between understanding something and accepting it? I think there is a difference. I understood Japanese culture. By marrying him, I accepted its terms. I knew perfectly well that there was no way he wouldn't have affairs—they all did, especially the wealthy ones. Divorce, at least at that time, was relatively rare. The stability of the family was what mattered.

When I finally filed for divorce decades later, Toshi didn't contest it. He begged our two sons to convince me not to go through with it—"I'll do anything"—but he wouldn't fight it publicly. He never showed up in court. The whole thing took thirty minutes. He signed everything over to me—the house, the cars.

***

The only time I ever saw Toshi cry was at my father's wake.

My father accepted Toshi for what he was. He loved him. He was kind. Then he did something that shouldn't have surprised me.

My father was the general superintendent of a large company that made airplane parts for the military. They were doing inventory control and needed people to count items on shelves—tedious, low-level work. My father proposed hiring Toshi.

I said, "You've got to be kidding. Toshi doesn't even know how to sweep a floor. He's never made himself a cup of tea."

But Toshi adored my father. So when my father proposed it, Toshi said yes. He did it. He started at the very bottom, and I'm proud of him for that.

Because of my father's position, he got Toshi into training programs—learning different skills, operating different machines. Toshi is very smart, and he rose quickly. When he needed a security clearance, he took the citizenship test and passed on the first try. Eventually, he became head of quality control for the whole company and worked there for many years.

Before he retired, they would call him at three in the morning on a Saturday if there was an emergency, if they had to get a part out to the military. He'd go in. They loved him because he was a typical Japanese worker—whatever needed to be done, he did. He never complained about the hours, the overtime, or anything.

I didn't go to his retirement party, but I saw videos of it. It was spectacular.

I think I understand now what the disinheritance actually meant to Toshi. In Japan, every aspect of his life had been controlled by family expectations. In America, even living in my father's house with almost no money, he had freedom—autonomy worth more than wealth.

My father gave him that. And when my father died, Toshi wept for what he had lost.

He still says to me, "I will always be grateful to you for bringing me to America."

In all our years—married, divorced, whatever we are now—he's never once said to me, "What did I give up to marry you?" Never. Not when we were living in my father's house with no money. Not when his family cut him off completely. Not when our marriage ended. He lost everything he'd been raised to inherit, and he's never held it against me.

***

Was it worth it? The $1.35 million per year the government spent on each of us?

That number astonished me when I finally learned it. We were already capped out on the federal pay scale—most of us were senior enough that we wouldn't make any more money. But the cost of keeping us there, providing us hazardous duty and wartime pay, the security convoys, the helicopters, the $5 million MRAPs, the biggest embassy ever built—the scale of it defied comprehension.

Compare that to the Peace Corps. That's expensive too, right? Training volunteers, sending them overseas. But then we're in-country for two years, living on a salary commensurate with the local economy, actually embedded in communities. Iraq was something else entirely. We'd been there since 2003, pouring money into an operation that felt increasingly like theater. The training they gave us—the evasive driving, the simulated attacks, language and culture lessons, firearm certification so we could carry a Glock—was about liability, not survival. And the government could say: Look what we provided. Look how we prepared them. Cover your ass. Absolutely.

But I'd seen government waste before. I knew what it looked like.

When I was in the Peace Corps, stationed in the Philippines, my stepmother Louise died of breast cancer, just as my mother had. That summer, I'd been sent to Zamboanga, the southernmost province, mostly Muslim, with no airport. So when the Peace Corps learned of her death, they sent a private plane to pick me up. It landed in a farmer's field.

I didn't ask for this. I had no say in it. All of a sudden, they said, "There's a plane in that field. Get on it. It's taking you to Manila, then Alaska, then Connecticut." Obviously, the government knew little or nothing about my family. Whatever my relationship with my stepmother was, my presence was important to my father and siblings, especially Joanne.

Was Iraq worth it? To me, absolutely. To the U.S., I have no idea. To the Iraqis I dealt with, I hope I was a positive influence. But could all that have happened without the massive embassy, the convoys, the huge financial investment per person? Probably not. The security apparatus made the work possible, even as it isolated us from the country we were supposed to be helping.

I understood all of this when I volunteered. So why did I go? Because we were already there. Because opposing the invasion didn't mean opposing every effort to help Iraqis rebuild. Because if I could do some good within a system I believed was fundamentally flawed, wasn't that better than doing nothing at all?

What I do know is this: I was there for a year. The Peace Corps plane that picked me up from that farmer's field—that was not a waste. Iraq? That's harder to say. The work mattered, even if the system that enabled it was bloated beyond reason.

***

People ask if Iraq transformed me. It's what memoirs are supposed to deliver—the before and after, the crucible that forges a new self.

But Iraq wasn't transformation. It was confirmation.

Confirmation of what I believed in, what I held to be true: that service matters even when the institutions meant to enable it fail you; that you can do the work without seeing the outcome; that democracy isn't something you impose—it's something people choose when the conditions allow. Those Iraqi law students arguing international law before judges from around the world, touring the Supreme Court, and sharing dinner with students from Afghanistan and Palestine—they clearly embraced democratic principles. The faculty at the law schools, the women in detention centers, even the police officer who corrected my understanding of the Quran—they weren't waiting for America to teach them about justice. They were waiting for the space to build their own.

The Peace Corps had taught me this decades earlier: you don't arrive to save people. You arrive to listen, to learn, and to offer your skills when they're wanted. The difference between the Peace Corps and Iraq was simple: we were invited to the Philippines. We imposed ourselves on Iraq.

What Iraq taught me is something I should have learned from the Derbacker case: you can follow every rule, document every step, have every court uphold your actions—and still be the villain in someone else's story. Bryson spelled out my name in his book. The media turned drug dealers into sympathetic grandparents. The narrative had already been decided.

America in Iraq was the same story, written larger. We came to build democracy. We spent billions. We trained police in forensics they might never use and taught constitutional law to judges who would never apply it. And to many Iraqis—maybe most—we were the people who'd destroyed their country and then occupied the rubble. The narrative was written before we arrived. Nothing we did was going to change it.

That's not an argument against trying. It's just a recognition that intent and perception are different things, and you don't get to control how your story is told.

The year I arrived in the Philippines, Marcos had just been elected president. I was a JFK fan, and many Peace Corps volunteers admired Marcos—thought he was the Philippine JFK. He was a graduate of the University of the Philippines. On the occasion of the university's founding, my housemate and I were invited to attend. I had a beautiful long gown made from piña cloth with a matching coat, my hair piled high. I got my picture taken with Imelda Marcos and her husband.

I was so proud of that photograph.

And then he became one of the most corrupt leaders in modern history: martial law, disappeared dissidents, billions stolen. Imelda's three thousand pairs of shoes became a symbol of plunder. It was so disappointing—that man I'd admired, that photograph I'd treasured. Iraq would teach me the same lesson.

And yet, within that imposition, within that massive embassy, there were still moments of genuine connection. Still spaces where something real could happen.

I learned that you can oppose a system while still doing good within it. That your complicity in something flawed doesn't eliminate your capacity for meaningful work. That sometimes the only honest response to institutional failure is to keep showing up anyway, doing what you can, where you are, with what you have.

***

What I want to be known for is simple: I tried hard. Whatever I undertook, I tried hard. I did my best. I didn't always succeed—no one always succeeds. But I think it's important to strive. There's a saying, maybe Michelangelo's: the tragedy isn't people striving and failing; it's not striving at all.

I want people to like me. I want people to love me. But I'm not going to compromise my integrity or my value system to get their love, friendship, or admiration. If doing what I think is right alienates people—if they think I'm too aggressive, too headstrong, too doctrinaire—that's hard to quantify as a cost.

Service is central to who I am: the Peace Corps, Africa, Bosnia, Bogotá, Iraq. When that email from the Attorney General asked for experienced attorneys to deploy to Baghdad, it took me ten seconds to say yes. Not because I was reckless or naive, but because I understood myself. This was the kind of work I was made for.

My son Cary asked why I would leave my beautiful house in Annapolis. My family thought I was crazy. Selfish. But the certainty I felt wasn't impulsive—it was the product of four decades of accumulated experience telling me exactly who I was.

Iraq confirmed it. The storage room had done what it was meant to do, even if the director never intended it that way. I felt sad. And then I got started.

***

Here's what I've learned about service, about a life lived on purpose: you don't start with Iraq. You start small. You start local. You tutor a kid at the library, serve meals at a shelter, or help an elderly neighbor with her taxes. You do it not because it will lead anywhere, but because you have something to give and someone needs it. Because those of us who grew up with advantages—a father who believed in us, an education, a country that let us become whatever we had the nerve to become—owe something back. The debt doesn't come with a payment plan. You just start paying.

And then something happens. Each small act of service teaches you something—about yourself, about other people, about what you're capable of. The tutoring leads to an after-school program. The shelter work connects you to housing advocacy. The neighbor introduces you to someone who needs a different kind of help. One thing opens into the next. Before you know it, you're raising your hand for the Peace Corps or applying to law school, or saying yes to Baghdad.

I didn't set out to live an adventurous life. I set out to be useful. The adventure came as a byproduct—the Philippines, Japan, Bosnia, Thailand, South Africa, Kenya, and Iraq. A life larger than anything I could have planned, built one small yes at a time—and on a government salary, which meant you got creative. Back when I was working in Japan, I bought a Pan Am around-the-world ticket for $1,000. You could circumnavigate the globe—start east, keep going east. As many stops as you wanted, up and down, as long as you kept moving in one direction. You had a year to use it. I didn't take a year—I was working—but I went to England, France, Italy, and India. And if you planned it right, which I did, you'd arrive at each stop around 6 p.m. No flights out that late, so the airline had to pay for your hotel and meals. Now that was living.

That's the secret no one tells you about service: it's not sacrifice. It's not noble self-denial. It's the surest path I know to a life that matters. You give, and somehow you receive more than you gave. You help, and somehow you become more than you were. You start small and local, and somehow you end up in places you never imagined, doing work you didn't know you were capable of, becoming a person you didn't know you could be.

If you're waiting for the right moment to start, this is it. If you're waiting until you have more time, more money, or more certainty, you'll wait forever. Start where you are. Start with what you have. Start small. The rest will follow.

***

I think about those Iraqi law students sometimes: the women from Baghdad who won their national rounds and their place in D.C.; the men from Thi-Qar who came in second. In ten years, twenty years, some of them will be judges, prosecutors, human rights lawyers. Those who came will remember arguing international law in Washington, touring the Supreme Court, and eating dinner with students from countries that were supposed to be enemies.

Will that make a difference? I don't know. I can't know. You plant seeds in impossible soil, and you walk away without any guarantee they'll grow. But you plant them anyway. My father understood that. He spent his whole life that way—raising kids with little help, believing that what you do matters even when you can't see the results.

I always think everything is going to work out just great for me, and everything has. That extends to our system too—I still have faith in it. Complicated faith earned the hard way. But faith, nonetheless.

The year I volunteered to handle immigration appellate work taught me why. Forty-five briefs, maybe fifty. Some pertained to people who'd fled the Soviet Union, Peru during the Shining Path years, places where government meant persecution. They had legitimate claims—every one of them. But they hadn't come forward when they arrived because they didn't trust the signs at the ports of entry: If you're fleeing persecution, there's a person here to help you. They may have seen those signs and thought, *It's a trap*. So they stayed silent, stayed hidden, and eventually the law caught up with them.

By then, they were employed, had started businesses, had jobs, had children, and spoke English. But the statute said: if the conditions from which you fled no longer exist—that is, there is no longer any danger that you will be persecuted—you must leave. The Soviet Union was gone. The Shining Path had been defeated. On paper, it was safe to go back.

I followed the law. I won every case. But the law doesn't always feel just, and I knew it. I'd like to see Congress fix it—give people who, in fact, had fled persecution, who've been here ten years, paying taxes, raising American children, a path forward. That wasn't my call to make. As an attorney, I uphold the law as written. If the law says go this way, I go that way, even when I disagree. That discipline is what makes the system worth defending.

And yet. We love our system. We love our society, with all its faults. That's the contradiction I've never fully resolved: believing deeply in what we have while understanding we can't give it to anyone else. They have to build it themselves, in their own way, in their own time.

I know I became the kind of lawyer my father could respect—one who refuses to argue what she doesn't believe, who takes the high road even when the institution makes it difficult, and who walks away from a thirty-two-year career rather than compromise her sense of what matters.

The storage room wasn't the ending; it was just where the institution thought my story stopped.

The real story—the one about choosing truth over comfort, about service as a way of life, and about understanding that not everything is personal betrayal—continues without them.

It always has.

THE RECORD

Leslie Cayer Ohta

Professional Experience
Resident Legal Advisor
February 2011 – March 2012
United States Department of Justice, Criminal Division
Overseas Prosecutorial Development Assistance and Training Program (OPDAT)
Provincial Reconstruction Team, Baghdad, Iraq

Responsible for advancing internationally accepted rule of law practices by supporting, advising, and training judges, lawyers, law students, police, and other legal entities involved in the enforcement of Iraq's laws. Goals included furthering the establishment of an independent judiciary; an effective and professional police force; detention practices that comport with human rights standards; and access to effective legal services. Additional goals included enhancing cooperation between Iraqi judges and police; greater use of forensic evidence; increasing security for judges; supporting juvenile detention facilities; and maximizing access to the legal system.

Specific projects included serving as National Administrator for Iraq for the Jessup International Law Moot Court Competition; Coordinator for the Iraqi High Tribunal; establishing a legal clinic at the Rusafa Women's Detention Facility; serving as the State Department's grant representative for a UNICEF Juvenile Detention Project; and lecturing at Al-Nahrain College of Law and the Rusafa Police Training Facility.

Trial Attorney
February 1995 – February 2011
United States Department of Justice, Civil Division
Commercial Litigation Branch, National Courts Section, Washington, D.C.

Represented the United States in cases involving contract disputes, including discovery, retaining experts, negotiating settlements, and trial; determined whether the Government should assert counterclaims in fraud, re-procurement costs, and damages. Member of the trial team representing the United States in *McDonnell Douglas and General Dynamics v. United States*, a multi-billion-dollar contract dispute arising out of the Navy's decision to terminate for default the contract to build the A-12, a Navy stealth attack plane. Primarily responsible for developing and presenting evidence, through expert witnesses, relating to stealth technology, program management, and the structure and propulsion system of the aircraft. Completed a one-year detail to the Office of Immigration Litigation, writing briefs and arguing appeals in asylum cases.

Security Clearance, Department of Justice: Top Secret, SCI

Assistant United States Attorney

August 1984 – February 1995

United States Attorney's Office, District of Connecticut, New Haven

Civil Litigation: medical malpractice, products liability, personal injury, environmental, employment discrimination, false claims, mail fraud, social security, constitutional torts, IRS summons enforcement, tax abatement, foreclosure, and habeas cases.

Criminal Prosecution: tax, bank fraud, extortion, bribery, wire fraud, mail fraud, tampering with a witness, interstate transportation of stolen property, false statements, postal theft, misapplication of bank funds, false claims, telemarketing fraud, and embezzlement cases.

Lead Attorney, Asset Forfeiture Unit: Headed the forfeiture program in Connecticut. Awarded the Prosecutor of the Year Award by the Association of Connecticut Chiefs of Police and the Milton S. Camilleri Distinguished Service Award from the Narcotics Enforcement Officers' Association.

Teaching: Lectured on forfeiture and polygraph issues to Assistant United States Attorneys and support staff in Washington, D.C., Phoenix, Tucson, Albuquerque, Miami, Kansas City, Atlanta, San Antonio, New Orleans, Nashville, and Orlando. Lectured to banking groups, bar associations, and local, state, and federal law enforcement agencies. Instructor at the Department of Justice Advocacy Institute: Civil Trial Practice and Forfeiture Trial Practice.

Trial Attorney
August 1980 – July 1984
United States Department of Justice, Civil Division, Torts Branch, Washington, D.C.

Nationwide trial litigation in federal courts in personal injury and wrongful death actions under the Federal Tort Claims Act and the Swine Flu Act; medical malpractice and products liability defense; extensive discovery and motion practice; complex multi-district litigation; appellate practice.

Law Clerk
June 1979 – July 1980
Associate Justice Joseph W. Bogdanski, Connecticut Supreme Court, Hartford

Legal Intern
June 1978 – August 1978
The Hartford Insurance Group, Hartford, Connecticut

Research Assistant and Investigator
September 1977 – January 1978
University of Connecticut School of Law, Criminal Clinic

Administrative Coordinator, Undergraduate Medical Education
June 1974 – June 1976
University of Connecticut Health Center, Farmington, Connecticut

Copy Editor
1970 – 1972
Sumitomo Electric Co., Osaka, Japan

English Teacher
1967 – 1972
YMCA, Osaka, Japan

United States Peace Corps
June 1965 – August 1967
Philippines

Chemistry and Physics Teacher, University of the Philippines Laboratory High School; developed curriculum materials in the Graduate School of Education, Quezon City. Physician's Aide, Rural Health Center, Ozamis City, Mindanao.

After Federal Service
Appointed Public Defender
December 2013 – August 2015
Connecticut Office of the Chief Public Defender

Represented indigent clients in criminal cases and parents and children in cases brought by the Department of Children and Families.

Faculty Member
September 2013 – January 2014
Norwalk Community College

Taught Constitutional Law.

Education

University of Connecticut School of Law

West Hartford, Connecticut

J.D. with Honors. Class Rank: Top 7% (11/156). Tied for highest score on the Connecticut Bar Examination.

Emmanuel College

Boston, Massachusetts

B.A., Major: Chemistry; Related Studies: Physics and Mathematics. Dean's List.

Honors and Awards

Prosecutor of the Year, Association of Connecticut Chiefs of Police, September 1991

Milton S. Camilleri Distinguished Service Award, Narcotics Enforcement Officers' Association, September 1993

Numerous U.S. Department of Justice Awards

Highest score (tied) on the Connecticut Multistate Bar Examination, July 1979

Articles selected for publication in the *Connecticut Law Review*: "Immunization Injuries: Proposed Compensatory Mechanisms, an Analysis," Vol. 11:1 (Fall 1978)

Represented the University of Connecticut School of Law in the Irving R. Kaufman National Moot Court Competition (securities law), New York, 1979

Hartford County Bar Association Scholarship, 1977–1978 and 1978–1979

Invited to lecture at the University of Minnesota Medical School on epidemiology in products liability cases

Citizenship Award, Glastonbury Democratic Town Committee, 2016

Litigation Experience
Trial Courts

United States District Courts for the District of Connecticut, Hawaii, Minnesota, Utah, North Dakota, South Dakota, Western District of Missouri, Northern District of New York, Western District of New York, Western District of Arkansas, District of Massachusetts, District of Vermont, and the Court of Federal Claims. Approximately 60 trials as lead counsel.

Appellate Courts

Court of Appeals for the District of Columbia Circuit, Eighth Circuit, Second Circuit, Ninth Circuit, and Court of Appeals for the Federal Circuit. Approximately 100 appeals.

Special Assistant United States Attorney, District of Vermont, District of Massachusetts, and Southern District of Florida.

Volunteer Experience
United Nations / OSCE Election Observer
May – September 1997
Bosnia-Herzegovina

Served as adjudicator determining eligibility of refugees to vote in municipal elections in Brcko, Republika Srpska. Investigated the politically motivated firing of a local election official, resulting in OSCE ordering her reinstatement. Co-authored the report of an investigation into fraud in the voter registration process, leading to OSCE voiding the non-refugee voter registration. Prepared training manual for voter registration staff. Served as polling station supervisor in Gradiska, Republika Srpska, September 1997.

Earthwatch Institute

Participated in scientific field research projects: archaeological dig, Thailand; Meerkat project, South Africa; water quality project, Czech Republic; elephant conservation project, Kenya (2019).

Sri Lanka Wildlife Conservation Society

Wild Elephant Conservation Project, 2016

Children of Hope Uganda

NGO promoting recovery and reintegration of children orphaned or formerly abducted by Joseph Kony's Lord's Resistance Army in northern Uganda. Annual travel to Uganda; conducted fundraisers in the United States.

Church Volunteer

Navajo Indian Reservation, construction project. Congregational Church of South Glastonbury: Syrian Refugee Committee, Social Action Committee, Missions Committee, Mission trip to Malawi (orphanage, HIV Clinic, and schools supported by the Church).

Community Organizations

Glastonbury Democratic Town Committee; Glastonbury Human Relations Commission; Glastonbury League of Women Voters; Glastonbury ABC Program, Board of Directors; Glastonbury MLK Community Initiative, former Co-President; Japan Society of Greater Hartford, former Executive Director and Secretary; US & Japan Society of CT, Board Member; TALK, Board Member, Social Justice Committee; Sheff Movement Coalition, Board of Directors.

Legal Volunteer Work

The Children's Law Center (Families in Transition Program; Truancy Intervention Project); Lawyers for Children America; Connecticut Veterans Legal Center; Glastonbury Rotary Club.

Polling Official

Book Judge, Annapolis, Maryland, numerous Presidential and midterm elections.

Languages

Latin, Esperanto, German, French, Filipino (Tagalog), Japanese, Spanish

Travel

Canada, Mexico, England, France (including Corsica), Italy, Switzerland, India, Thailand, Indonesia, Singapore, Hong Kong, Philippines, Korea, Japan, New Zealand, Australia, Austria, Greece, Turkey, Bosnia-Herzegovina, Croatia, Russia, Moldova, Ukraine, Transnistria, Germany, South Africa, Botswana, Zimbabwe, Czech Republic, Wales, Scotland, Northern Ireland, Republic of Ireland, Malta, Spain, Jordan, Kuwait, Kenya, Egypt, Iraq, Uganda, Rwanda, Sri Lanka, Malawi

SOURCES AND FURTHER READING

The events in this memoir are drawn from firsthand experience, contemporaneous emails, and official documents. The following sources shaped or appear in the narrative and offer readers a way deeper into the history, law, and policy that framed a year in Baghdad.

Books

Benedict, Ruth. *The Chrysanthemum and the Sword: Patterns of Japanese Culture*. Houghton Mifflin, 1946.

Written during World War II by an anthropologist who had never visited Japan, this study of Japanese culture and psychology became the blueprint for the American occupation. MacArthur's administration followed its analysis so closely—preserving the Emperor, maintaining existing social structures, putting chocolate bars in soldiers' hands—that Japan's transition became one of the most peaceful in modern history. The contrast with Iraq haunts this memoir.

Bryson, Bill. *I'm a Stranger Here Myself: Notes on Returning to America After Twenty Years Away*. Broadway Books, 1999.

Bryson's popular column collection about readjusting to American life includes a chapter on civil asset forfeiture in which he holds up Leslie Ohta by name as an example of prosecutorial overreach. He never contacted her for comment. The passage, and what it got wrong, is discussed in Chapter 3.

Laws and International Agreements

United Nations Protocol to Prevent, Suppress and Punish Trafficking in Persons (the "Palermo Protocol"). UN General Assembly, 2000.

The first international instrument to define human trafficking, the Palermo Protocol established the "3P" framework—prevention, prosecution, and victim protection—that became the global standard. Iraq had signed related documents without passing implementing legislation, a contradiction that Leslie worked to resolve during her deployment. Full text available through the UN Office on Drugs and Crime: unodc.org.

Trafficking Victims Protection Act (TVPA). Public Law 106-386, U.S. Congress, 2000.

The U.S. statute that gave the Palermo Protocol its teeth: no American foreign aid could flow to any country that failed to prohibit human trafficking. This leverage was Leslie's primary tool in roundtable negotiations at the American Embassy compound—leverage that a decade of funding workarounds had rendered largely theoretical. Full text at govinfo.gov.

United Nations Convention on the Rights of the Child (UNCRC). UN General Assembly, 1989.

Iraq had signed the UNCRC, but the treatment of children in its criminal justice system—children as young as nine held criminally responsible, lengthy pretrial detention, no rehabilitation—violated both its provisions and Iraq's own domestic law. The gap between signature and reality was the subject of Leslie's juvenile justice work and her contribution to the State Department's annual human rights report. Full text at ohchr.org.

UN Standard Minimum Rules for the Administration of Juvenile Justice ("The Beijing Rules"). UN General Assembly Resolution 40/33, 1985.

The international framework governing how states should treat young people in conflict with the law. Leslie reviewed these rules alongside the UNCRC when preparing her juvenile justice assignment; they formed the baseline against which she documented Iraq's actual practices. Available at unodc.org.

Iraq Juvenile Care Law No. 76 of 1983. Republic of Iraq.

Iraq's own domestic juvenile justice statute—which its detention system was also failing to follow. Part of what made Leslie's reporting assignment so striking was that the problem was not simply a gap between international standards and local law, but between local law and local practice.

Reports and Official Documents

U.S. Department of State. *Country Reports on Human Rights Practices.* Annual. state.gov/reports/human-rights-reports.

Published annually for virtually every country, these reports—prepared by U.S. diplomatic staff—carry real policy consequences: foreign aid, sanctions, and asylum determinations all draw on them. Leslie contributed the section on juvenile detention to the Iraq report for the year she was deployed. Readers interested in conditions on the ground during 2011–2012 can consult the Iraq report for those years at state.gov.

U.S. Department of State. *Trafficking in Persons Report.* Annual. state.gov/trafficking-in-persons-report.

A separate annual report tracking each country's compliance with anti-trafficking standards, with tier rankings tied to foreign assistance eligibility. Iraq's repeated failure to pass implementing legislation while continuing to receive U.S. funding is the subject of Chapter 11. The report's eventual addition of the United States as a subject country—a development Leslie found genuinely shocking—reflects how much the issue had grown domestically.

UNAMI/OHCHR. *Report on Human Rights in Iraq: January–June 2011.* United Nations Assistance Mission for Iraq, 2011. ohchr.org.

The UN's own mid-year assessment of human rights conditions in Iraq during Leslie's deployment, drawing on direct monitoring by UNAMI and reporting from civil society and NGOs. Leslie circulated this report to family and friends in a contemporaneous email, noting: "Wish there was more good news to report."

Articles

The following articles were sent by Leslie to family and friends during her deployment, as supplementary context for her emails from Baghdad. Several original URLs are no longer live; publication information is provided for archival research.

Al Arabiya News. "Iraq Doctors Targeted; Healthcare System in Crisis." April 9, 2011.

A report on the ongoing targeting of Iraqi medical professionals and academics following the 2003 invasion, noting that before the war, Iraq had been a regional leader in healthcare and higher education. Leslie forwarded this piece as background for the deteriorating professional class she encountered in Baghdad.

Staff Writers. "Killers Target Iraq's Ravaged Elite Again." *UPI / Space War*. April 11, 2011.

A follow-on UPI report covering the murder of an Iraqi surgeon and a university researcher, and the re-escalation of violence against professionals who had begun returning to Iraq after the 2009 security surge. One of several dispatches Leslie sent home illustrating the fragility of any progress she was witnessing.

Niqash. "Female Judges: Still Second Class in Iraqi Courts." *Niqash.org*, 2011.

Reporting on the underrepresentation of women in senior judicial positions in Iraq, featuring female judges describing their own marginalization. Leslie followed conditions for women in the legal system closely—both because of her rule-of-law work and because it was the world she herself inhabited.

Murray, Rebecca. "Female Trafficking Soars in Iraq." *IPS News*. August 28, 2011. Originally published at ipsnews.net.

An IPS investigation into the epidemic of prostitution and sex trafficking in post-invasion Iraq, arguing that military occupation and sectarian violence had shattered national institutions and displaced millions, creating the conditions for mass exploitation. Leslie forwarded this article the same week she was beginning to document trafficking conditions for the State Department's annual report.

The Jessup Competition

Philip C. Jessup International Law Moot Court Competition. International Law Students Association. jessup.org.

Founded in 1959 and named for former U.S. Supreme Court Justice Philip C. Jessup, this is the world's largest moot court competition, with participants from over 100 countries annually. Law school teams research and argue both sides of a hypothetical international law dispute before judges drawn from the bench and bar. Leslie competed in the Jessup as a law student, and decades later found herself organizing Baghdad College of Law's first-ever participation from a war zone—an experience that became the emotional center of her deployment.

ACKNOWLEDGEMENTS

To all the hero's and miscreants who have so enriched my life, thank you!

To my father, Leslie Morrison Cayer; husband, Toshi Ohta; sons, Cary Leslie and Miki James; and siblings, Joanne Cayer Labriola, Marilyn Louise Cayer, and David Allen Cayer.

www.ingramcontent.com/pod-product-compliance
Lightning Source LLC
LaVergne TN
LVHW100303210926
848480LV00003B/1010